I live in a lovely village!

With trees, mountains, lakes and rivers …

A wondrous paradise …

Where everyone is treated equally …

Where no one is harassed …

Where the law applies to everyone …

Davide Burke

Index   **Page**

Chapter 1 – Part 1

A village where the leader is wise and good!

As cited:

There are people who have a bit of the Hitler complex and have managed to get themselves elected to the executive!

One who has a Hitler complex does not allow the people we voted in to represent to do their job.

What is with the dictator garbage??

No one would say this about our village leader?

A Portrait of the Visual Arts in Canada

http://fredericks-artworks.blogspot.ca/2012_06_01_archive.html

And, here's a reader comment to prove my point:

rorrfs → Shana Carquez · 2 years ago

Relax conbots, no need for such vicious attacks. Art is supposed to evoke emotion, stir a response, generate debate. The artist has accomplished all this in spades. Nice job Margaret!

Chapter 2

A village where the leader is not evil or bad!

As cited:

"When Stars new album The North came out earlier this fall, outspoken singer Torquil Campbell made any number of political pronouncements to the press, right up to warning about Canada's creeping fascism.

Yeah, yeah. He's an evil person. He's a bad person."[1]

As cited:

The stepped-up authoritarian, anti-democratic manner Stephen Harper conducts himself since obtaining his Parliamentary majority nine months ago raises serious concerns about how far right he is planning to push the country in his effort to forever change the face of Canada. [2]

Harper hates many things about Canada—most of all the moderate liberalism that a majority of people have preferred over the years. He has adopted a 'take-no-prisoners' attitude, rushing ahead with destructive plans never before discussed in public, as well as doubling cuts to government compared to what he said before the election. [3]

Elected with the support of only 25 per cent of eligible voters, Harper nevertheless is running roughshod over the wishes and interests of the majority 75 per cent of Canadians. [4]

Here's a Fascist Principle - Disdain for the importance of human rights.

And, as further cited:

The regimes viewed human rights as of little value and a hindrance to realizing the objectives of the ruling elite. Through clever use of propaganda, the population was brought to accept these human rights abuses by marginalizing, even demonizing, those being targeted. When abuse was egregious, the tactic was to use secrecy, denial, and disinformation.[5]

Our village leader would never fit this bill?

As further noted, you decide:

Jack Etkin, The Bridge, B.C., March 2011: "Mr. Harper is very likely a war criminal. In Afghanistan, he has forced Canadian troops to give innocent civilians to the Afghan police to be tortured. That is a war crime, but it is never mentioned by the corporate media." [6]

Alex Neve, The Toronto Star, January 3, 2011: "At the end of the day, what transpired within the official summits was overshadowed by the staggering assault on freedom of expression that played out on the streets of Toronto. It still seems impossible to imagine that more than 1,100 people were arrested over the weekend, the overwhelming majority of whom were involved in peaceful acts of protest or were just passing by. [7]

Susan Riley, Ottawa Citizen, January 27, 2012: "He (Harper) was never going to downplay China's human rights abuses in the name of the "almighty dollar," until it became useful to ardently court China as a customer for tars and oil." [8]

Our village police would never do this would they?

"Nothing will happen to them, still they are on the job, the four RCMP officers who caused Robert's death by what they did, and then they lie," said Cisowski [see Appendix, cited below].[9]

Richmond RCMP Sgt. Pierre Lemaitre said officers struggled to subdue the man: 'Even though he had received what they call pulses, two pulses from Taser, he was still out of control.'[10]

The man actually died after 4 Taser jolts, witness alleges.[11]

In fact, one witness said she offered to tell the RCMP officers what she witnessed, and that one officer said, "'I'll be with you in a few minutes.'" But the officers did not take a statement from her, she alleges.[12]

As reported, "within seconds, he had been Tasered. Dziekanski, even after falling to the ground, shrieking in pain, was Tasered repeatedly."[13]

Our village police would never do this would they?

"After the event, the Mounties all gave similar statements about how Dziekanski had come at them, yelling and wildly swinging the stapler, and how several officers had to wrestle the man to the ground."[14]

However, a video proves the RCMP officers outright lied!

A witness's video of the event showed none of that happened ... if not for the video, might have got away with whitewashing what the judge called the force's "shameful" conduct in the events that led to an innocent man's death.[15]

As further reported, "I saw more RCMP officers lie to cover up this cowardly crime."[16]

Incredibly, "on Dec. 12, 2008, B.C. Criminal Justice branch spokesman Stan Lowe "cleared" the four officers of any wrongdoing and portrayed Dziekanski as a violent and agitated alcoholic whose irrational behavior contributed to his own death."[17]

However, even this Stan Lowe was put in his place when Cisowski had the satisfaction of hearing Thomas Braidwood call the four Mounties "inapproviately aggressive" and "patently unbelievable," while emphasizing Dziekanski did nothing wrong nor in any way caused his own death.[18]

Caught in their lies thanks to videotape of the "cowardly" crime, as it has been described.

Braidwood called the bystander video by Paul Pritchard of Dziekanski's Tasering death "invaluable" evidence that "couldn't be cross-examined."[19]

"Onlookers were incredulous when RCMP Commissioner William Elliott said Friday he wouldn't be announcing any disciplinary measures for any of the four Mounties for their role in Dziekanski's death."[20]

Get away with murder and no consequences?

Even the apology to Robert Dziekanski's mother was a bunch of RCMP bunk?

"A raft of internal RCMP emails was released through an Access to Information Act request showing that the April 1 apology was a carefully-crafted script designed not to blame any RCMP member."[21]

"On the day before the staging of the apology, RCMP Deputy Commissioner Gary Bass reassured RCMP staff relations supervisor Brian Roach that their "apology" to Cisowski did not mean they were apologizing for anything specific that any of their officers had done."[22]

"Essentially, even though the word 'apology' worries some, we are not apologizing for the actions of specific members or saying anything about specific actions."[23]

Cisowski said yesterday "this just shows that the RCMP even when they apologize to me, they coverup."[24]

Actually tasered five times!

"The e-mail, sent by RCMP Chief Supt. Dick Bent to Assistant Commissioner Al Macintyre suggested for the first time that the four Mounties who responded to a call at Vancouver's airport planned to use a Taser on Robert Dziekanski, who died at the airport on Oct. 14, 2007, after he was Tasered five times."[25]

Our village leader would never fit this bill?

http://fredericks-artworks.blogspot.ca/2012_06_01_archive.html

And, here's a reader comment to prove my point:

 kootenayredneck → Danielle Kennedy · 2 years ago
I believe it's 2012 not 1950. So what if the limp dic-tator is shown in the nude,
Burt Reynolds did it years ago.

Just wander back to church and confess your sinful thoughts.

Footnotes

1. *Stars' Torquil Campbell Calls Stephen Harper 'An Evil Man,' Talks Politics And Pop Music*, By Joshua Ostroff, Huffington Post Canada, Posted: 11/22/2012

2 - 8. *Is Stephen Harper displaying fascist-like tendencies?*
Canadian Dimension, Canadian Politics, Economy and Foreign Policy, Web Exclusive,
By Nick Fillmore, February 8th 2012

9. *Still they get no consequences.* By Suzanne Fournier, The Province, June 20, 2010.

10 – 11. *RCMP say deceased man was 40-year-old Polish immigrant Robert Dziekanski.*
Last Updated: Tuesday, October 16, 2007. CBC News.

12. *One witness said she offered to tell the RCMP officers what she witnessed.*

13 - 15. *Inquiry deservedly hammers RCMP in Dziekanski death.* By Paul Schneiderit,
The Chronicle Herald, Tue. Jun 22.

16. *I saw more RCMP officers lie to cover up this cowardly crime.*

17 - 20. *Still they get no consequences.* By Suzanne Fournier, The Province, June 20, 2010.

21 - 24. *RCMP's apology grudging, evasive.* By Suzanne Fournier, The Province, June 17, 2010.

25. *E-mail Suggests Four RCMP Officers Committed Perjury While Senior Officers Sat Silent.* Contributed on Sun, 2009/06/21 - 2:30pm.

Also see: *Startling New Email Halts Inquiry.* By Neal Hall and Lori Culbert; June 20, 2009 - Vancouver Sun.

Also see: *Damning e-mail suggests the four officers committed perjury and that senior officers sat silent while they did.* By Ian Mulgrew; June 20, 2009 - Vancouver Sun.

Coroners' Report

British Columbia, Canada - Ministry of Justice
CORONER'S REPORT
INTO THE DEATH OF
CBse No.: 2007-0270-1054
ROBERT DZIEKANSKI OF POLAND

ClASSIFICATION OF DEATH HOMICIDE
Date Signed: MARCH 20,2013

I, Patrick Cullinane, a Coroner in the Province of British Columbia, have investigated the death of the above named, which was reported to Kate Corcoran on the 14th day of October, 2007/ and as a result of such investigation have determined the following facts and circumstances:

Mr. Dziekanski entered the semi-secure International Reception Lounge at 12:40 a.m. on October 14,2007. As noted Mr. Dziekanski spoke no English and at this point had been inside the airport for almost ten hours. At this time Mr. Dziekanski appeared to be exhibiting behaviours that might best be described as agitated and flustrated. While several witnesses described Mr. Dziekanski' s obvious upset, none identified feeling threatened by him.

Due to Mr. Dziekanski's perceived state of agitation, security personnel from the airpport and members of the airport Royal Canadian Mounted Police [RCMP] detachment were dispatched.

The RCMP officers arrived at I :28 a.m.

The RCMP officers deployed a conducted energy weapon within 30 seconds from the time when one of the officers attending the scene first spoke to Mr. Dziekanski, ultimately deploying the weapon five times.

Subsequently, the officers restrained Mr. Dziekanksi and handcuffed him. In addition to the statements by various witnesses who observed the interaction between Mr. Dziekanski and the RCMP members, the events were also recorded on video taken by another passenger in the airport terminal.

Within seconds of being handcuffed Mr. Dziekanski lay motionless on the floor and was breathing heavily. He soon became unconscious and it was apparent he was experiencing significant medical distress.

RCMP members did not engage in any resuscitation efforts but requested an ambulance be dispatched. The call to the BC Ambulance Service (BCAS) occurred at I :32 a.m. and Richmond Fire-Rescue also received a dispatch call at I :34 a.m.

Richmond Fire and Rescue arrived at the scene at approximately I :42 a.m. and the first two BCAS paramedics arrived at the scene approximately 90 seconds later.

Roughly one minute later advanced life support paramedics also arrived at the scene, at which point they found Mr. Dziekanski's face was bluish.

When Richmond Fire-Rescue staff first arrived, Mr. Dziekanski was lying in a prone position, with his hands handcuffed behind his back.

In order to assist in assessing his condition the RCMP members were requested to remove the handcuffs, but this request was declined by the RCMP officers.

Mr. Dziekanski was pronounced dead at the scene!!!

Appendix

'Still they get no consequences'

'Still they get no consequences'
Four Mounties involved should not get off scot-free, says Dziekanski's mother
By Suzanne Fournier, The Province June 20, 2010

Zofia Cisowski's "darkest hour" after learning that her son Robert Dziekanski was dead came when B.C. criminal justice officials declared that the RCMP had done nothing wrong -- and that it was her son's own fault that he died.

Now that she has been vindicated by the Braidwood Inquiry report castigating the officers and ruling her son did nothing wrong, Cisowski still carries with her a news clipping containing the earlier blaming, hurtful words.

On Dec. 12, 2008, B.C. Criminal Justice branch spokesman Stan Lowe "cleared" the four officers of any wrongdoing and portrayed Dziekanski as a violent and agitated alcoholic whose irrational behaviour contributed to his own death.

Last week, Walter Kosteckyj, Cisowski's lawyer, said "that was Zofia's darkest hour, after losing her son, and that's why she still carries that news clipping with her."

So far, Cisowski notes, none of the four Mounties "has ever got any consequences."

On Friday, Cisowski had the satisfaction of hearing Thomas Braidwood call the four Mounties "inapproprivately aggressive" and "patently unbelievable," while emphasizing Dziekanski did nothing wrong nor in any way caused his own death.

"This tragic case is at its heart the story of shameful conduct by a few officers," Braidwood said.

"It ought not to reflect unfairly on the many thousands of RCMP and other police officers who have protected our communities and earned a well-deserved reputation in doing so."

Cisowski heard B.C. Attorney-General Mike de Jong promise to appoint a special prosecutor and commit to a citizen-led Independent Investigation

Office to conduct criminal investigations into RCMP or municipal police incidents causing death or harm.

Friday was an exhausting day after a night in which Cisowski slept little, coming at the end of years of hearings in which a video of her son's death was screened repeatedly -- although it helped a kind and patient former judge get to the truth.

Braidwood called the bystandervideo by Paul Pritchard of Dziekanski's Tasering death "invaluable" evidence that "couldn't be cross-examined."

Cisowski received an apology Friday from the RCMP's top cop, Commissioner William Elliott.

Yet as a mother, Cisowski did not hear from Elliott -- the first lawyer and non-cop to head the national RCMP -- the words she has waited so long to hear, she said.

"Nothing will happen to them, still they are on the job, the four policemen who caused Robert's death by what they did, and then they lie," said Cisowski.

Listening to Elliott say the RCMP has reformed its training and Taser policies, Cisowski whispered: "Still they get no consequences for causing my son's death."

Braidwood's 460-page report, entitled simply Why? The Robert Dziekanski Tragedy, is a blistering denunciation of the four Mounties who Tasered and restrained Dziekanski face down, then left him unattended until he died.

Onlookers were incredulous when Elliott said Friday he wouldn't be announcing any disciplinary measures for any of the four Mounties for their role in Dziekanski's death. He said he would await the special prosecutor's report.

Elliott acknowledged that Cpl. Benjamin Monty Robinson is suspended with pay, but only in connection with the unrelated traffic death of a motorcyclist. That matter doesn't go to trial until April 2011.

The other three -- Const. Gerry Rundel, Const. Bill Bentley and Const. Kwesi Millington -- are "on the job but not in front-line policing," said Elliott, who couldn't explain why the four officers could be criticized about an unjustified death and yet remain on the RCMP payroll.

Elliott hinted it might even be too late to mete out internal punishment, but admitted: "We recognize there needs to be fairly fundamental changes in our discipline system."

Braidwood said the four Mounties behaved as if they were responding to a "barroom brawl," and senior officer Robinson "intervened in an inapprovisately aggressive manner."

"I found that Mr. Dziekanski had been compliant, was not defiant or resistant, did not brandish the stapler and did not move toward any of the officers," Braidwood said.

"I concluded the constable [Millington] was not justified in deploying the weapon and neither the constable nor the corporal honestly perceived that Mr. Dziekanski was intending to attack any of the officers."

Braidwood said the other two officers also "offered patently unbelievable after-the-fact rationalizations of their police notes and statements to [the Integrated Homicide Investigation Team]."

As for Robinson's claim that the Mounties made a point to check if Dziekanski was alive, Braidwood was dismissive.

"I can place little reliance on the testimony of Cpl. Robinson that he constantly monitored Mr. Dziekanski's breathing until the firefighters arrived. Similarly, I find unpersuasive the testimony of Const. Rundel that . . . he knelt down near Mr. Dziekanski and heard him breathing and snoring.

"I am satisfied that Mr. Dziekanski went into cardiac arrest first, then went unconscious, and finally showed signs of cyanosis, all within 75 seconds of being handcuffed."

De Jong was prompt to appoint special prosecutor Richard Peck to look into possible criminal charges against the four Mounties.

"There was misconduct here and that reflects badly [on the RCMP]," said de Jong.

"The human dimension in this is staggering, that someone would be lost within an airport for hours, separated by a glass door forever from one of his loved ones."

The stark images on the Pritchard film, of the police behaviour and a man's death, had enormous impact, said De Jong.

"Many people [not just in B.C.] remember where they were at the time the film was shown," he said.

"We are welcoming and one of the friendliest countries in the world -- we didn't display it that day."

Chapter 1 – Part 3

A village where the leader is fair and open!

As mentioned:

Under some of the regimes, the mass media were under strict direct control and could be relied upon never to stray from the party line. Other regimes exercised more subtle power to ensure media orthodoxy. Methods included the control of licensing and access to resources. The leaders of the mass media were often politically compatible with the power elite. The result was usually success in keeping the general public unaware of the regimes' excesses.[1]

And this surely is the case with Canadian Prime Minister Stephen Harper!

Here's another Fascist Principle - A controlled mass media.

As further cited:

Lawrence Martin, iPolitics, December 2, 2011: "Central to right-wing nationalism is information control and it is one of this government's major priorities. A vetting system of unprecedented scope requires all communications to be filtered through central command. Much is done to limit access to information in a government often criticized for its secrecy. Fifteen hundred communications officers are at work massaging the message to fit the governing agenda. Bureaucrats, including those at the Privy Council Office are pressured into becoming propagandists."[2]

Nick Fillmore blog, A Different Point of View… January 11, 1012: "First of all, newspaper corporations strongly support and benefit from neoliberal policies. Second, it appears that all major media companies in the country, with the exception of The Toronto Star, are on the Harper bandwagon. Many of the dailies occasionally criticize Harper for one thing or another, but to allow any of their journalists to describe Harper's neoliberal policies in full would enrage the vindictive Harper. It also would send an alert to a public that does not realize that many of the things they dislike about the Conservatives are part of a bigger bundle."[3]

And, that is why the main newspapers / news media in Canada searched all the video tapes at the Vancouver, British Colombia, Canada airport to come up with the worst picture of the poor Polish immigrant, Robert Dziekanski, tasered to death within 30 seconds by the Royal Canadian Mounted Police:

THE VANCOUVER SUN

Robert Dziekanski holds a small table at the Vancouver Airport before he was tasered by police in this image from video. The BC Coroner's Service says the death of Polish immigrant Dziekanski in an altercation with RCMP officers at Vancouver's airport six years ago was a homicide.

NATIONAL POST

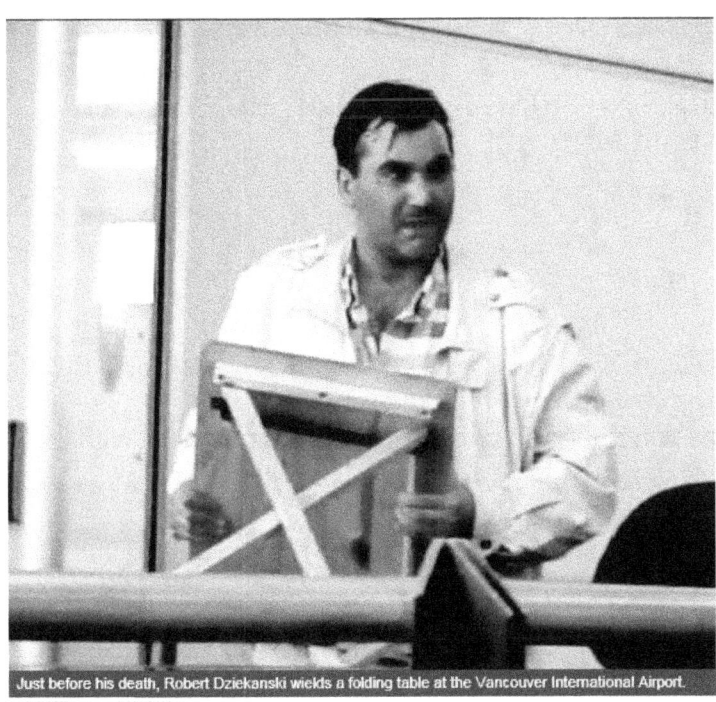

Just before his death, Robert Dziekanski wields a folding table at the Vancouver International Airport.

And once again, thanks to the main newspapers / news media in Canada, it's very clear they all searched the video tapes at the Vancouver, British Colombia, Canada airport to come up with the worst picture of this poor Polish immigrant:

CBCnews | British Columbia

Robert Dziekanski holds a small table at the Vancouver airport before he was stunned with a Taser by police in this image from video. The B.C. Coroner's Service says the death of the Polish immigrant six years ago was a homicide. (Paul Pritchard/Canadian Press)

SIMPLY SHOWS THERE'S NOTHING BUT "SCUM" RUNNING THE CANADIAN MAINSTREAM MEDIA!!!

JUST TO SUPPORT THE RCMP CALLOUS MURDER OF THIS POOR IMMIGRANT TO CANADA!!

Footnotes

1 - 3. Is Stephen Harper displaying fascist-like tendencies?
Canadian Dimension, Canadian Politics, Economy and Foreign Policy, Web Exclusive, By Nick Fillmore, February 8th 2012

Chapter 4

A village where the leader doesn't mistreat women!

And, as further reported:

Beyond the simple fact that the political elite and the national culture were male-dominated, these regimes inevitably viewed women as second-class citizens. They were adamantly anti-abortion and also homophobic. These attitudes were usually codified in Draconian laws that enjoyed strong support by the orthodox religion of the country. [1]

Here's another Fascist Principle - Rampant sexism.

As further noted, you decide:

Laura Wood, rabble.ca, January 24, 2011: "Harper dramatically cut the funding of what was Canada's most important body for promoting gender equity, Status of Women Canada. Status of Women Canada provided advocacy, research and lobbying on behalf of women's groups. The government closed 12 out of 16 regional offices of SWC and their operating budget was cut by 38 per cent. Changes were imposed to the criteria for funding for the Status of Women Canada's Women's Program that essentially barred advocacy and lobbying groups from receiving funding." [2]

Informal Feminism blog, February 27, 2011: "Another large change that Harper made was to cut the plans for a government funded daycare program. This is a program that had been in the works before Harper was elected to office, it allotted 5 billion dollars to fund a government run daycare program for Canadian families. Harper pulled this plan from the table and replaced it with a 2.6 billion dollar plan, which instead sends $100 dollars a month to Canadian families with children under six. This change in the plans was very dramatic and is another way that Harper's conservative views are affecting women in Canada. By getting rid of the 5 billion dollar plan it makes it harder for women to return to the workforce full-time if that is what they want or need to do." [3]

Is that why the female RCMP officers sexually abused and molested by some of the male RCMP officers, including some high up in the organization are not getting anywhere with their law suits??

As cited, "there's been little said or done to date that should give the public confidence action will be taken to root out harassment in the RCMP. In fact, the response to the ever-widening scandal has been deeply discouraging." [4]

"Bob Paulson, the Mounties' new Commissioner, has made stern-faced avowals to get to the heart of the matter and take a zero-tolerance approach to harassment going forward. But anyone who has bullied or harassed (sexually or otherwise) a colleague up to now would appear to be off the hook." [5]

On Friday, CBC's the fifth estate revisited the case of RCMP Staff Sergeant Robert Blundell, who in 2001 admitted to "discreditable conduct," in connection with allegations that he sexually harassed and assaulted two female officers in the late 1990s.[6]

"The program revealed how the two women – Krista Carle and Victoria Cliffe – were devastated when an internal hearing into the charges was brought to an unexpected conclusion. What happened? A high-ranking RCMP official intervened and got the accused to admit to certain facts that the two officers say grossly understated the actual offences."[7]

In the end, the onetime undercover cop admitted to "touching the private areas" on top of the clothing of one of the women and grabbing the breast of the other. He was ordered to take counselling and was docked a day's pay. Staff Sgt. Blundell was subsequently promoted and still works in the force.[8]

"There are a number of things about this case that should disturb us all."[9]

"Firstly, the high-ranking Mountie who brokered the unusual and highly contentious Blundell plea deal was Peter German. (The accused had denied all charges against him at a previous hearing). Mr. German is a deputy commissioner of the RCMP and was a finalist for the commissioner's job given to Mr. Paulson. He does not come out looking at all good in the fifth estate's story and now he is a member of the senior management team pledging to clean this harassment mess up."[10]

"The new Commissioner, Bob Paulson, meantime told the fifth estate that he considers the Blundell matter closed – permanently."[11]

Author's note: Way to go Paulson – leave a "sexual pervert" in the RCMP!

Not only that – promote him!

Paulson is nothing but a joke?

And, it appears this article agrees?

"That's wrong. He should reopen the case immediately. Even based on the charges that Staff Sgt. Blundell agreed to – which, as mentioned, the female officers involved say vastly diminishes what happened – he should have been kicked out of the force. He still should be."[12]

"But if the Blundell matter is considered spilled milk, what does that mean for previous incidents of harassment that may come to light in the future?"[13]

"How can the new Commissioner allow one person to go virtually unpunished – and, in fact, be promoted – and then come down hard on others whose past behaviour is found to be wanting as a result of various reviews and investigations now under way?"[14]

Author's note: Not another "frigging" RCMP bully?

Didn't the RCMP have enough of that with the last "jack-ass" RCMP Commissioner, William Elliott?

"There are some, including Darryl Davies, a criminology professor at Carleton University, who believe that Commissioner Paulson should temporarily step aside until bullying allegations levelled against him are cleared up."[15]

"Those claims were made by Canadian diplomat Robert Fowler who wrote in Season in Hell that a senior Mountie – since identified as the new Commissioner – bullied Mr. Fowler's wife while he was a 130-day captive of an al-Qaeda affiliate in West Africa."[16]

Author's note: What, what a "slug"!

"This is a serious charge that should be investigated," said Prof. Davies. "There were other people in the room when Mr. Paulson spoke to Fowler's wife. What do they have to say about what happened? It shouldn't be hard to find out.[17]

"We have a crippled and dysfunctional organization under attack for bullying and harassment in the system and now we have a commissioner who has a cloud over his head related to this very issue of bullying and it hasn't been cleared up."[18]

"This is a horrible situation that seems to get bigger by the day," said the professor. "And it should go to a royal commission or public inquiry. That's the only way you'll get to the bottom of what is going on here."[19]

"He's right, of course. As it is, few officers are likely to pay a price for their role in potentially one of the worst scandals to ever hit the force."[20]

Reader's comments:

Creef
5:02 AM on December 13, 2011

Uneducated, power-hungry ignoramuses who can commit crimes with impunity.

George Nikitin
12:23 PM on December 13, 2011

The RCMP murders with relative impunity (Robert Dziekanski, Ian Bush, etal.), so harassment, while still egregious, is somewhat lower on the list of issues that need addressing.

Rusherman
12:14 AM on December 13, 2011

Old boys at the Old Boy Club. Nothing new but a bit of spun rhetoric for the masses. By the way does in not bother anybody but me that this organization with so many perverts found dealing with each other on the inside are the same people who carry guns and other weapons out in the public. That they are the law on the streets. If you want to worry about anyone worry about the citizens that come under their power on a daily basis.

Bookgoalie
1:06 AM on December 13, 2011

What came out at me the most with the Fifth Estate piece was how Paulson is certainly not the right person to change the culture of the Mounties. He started out the tense and defensive interview by stating that overall his force has "a very good record" when dealing with these matters. Is he kidding? Also, what was being alledged was very serious criminal behaviour and Paulson spouts off some banality that the 1 day suspension was indeed a heavy hit for Blundell. Why? Because the discipline stopped him from becoming an inspector? Did I hear him right? If Blundell is as alleged, guilty of these acts, the guy belongs in jail, not simply prevented from being "promoted." How can any policeman in good conscience defend this?

Statler Waldorf
5:42 AM on December 13, 2011

Paulson was the wrong choice. Another BC old boys club guy who will be in over his head in no time.

Ken K1
1:12 AM on December 13, 2011

Wow, what a shock. It hasn't even taken a month for the new Chief to become one of the suspected wrongdoers that he is supposed to be rooting out of the force. They are trained to be bullies; what do you expect? And how can anyone be surprised he is taking the stance that an old case is permanently closed - a case that sounds an awful like a criminal offence and not just sexual harassment. Can't you just feel the ranks closing? Paulson wants to get to the bottom of the problem but doesn't want to upset those in the ranks. That is simply a cover up.

Andrea_W
11:39 PM on December 12, 2011

*Cpl. Catherine Galliford, who was the RCMP spokeswoman on the Air India and Pickton investigations, said police could have obtained a search warrant for convicted serial killer Robert Pickton **YEARS before they arrested the B.C. pig farmer.*

R. Hebner
9:30 PM on December 12, 2011

For the uninitiated, Canadian Prime Minister Mr Harper changes Commissioners every time the seat gets a little too warm from too many issues.

Footnotes

1 - 3. Is Stephen Harper displaying fascist-like tendencies?
Canadian Dimension, Canadian Politics, Economy and Foreign Policy, Web Exclusive, By Nick Fillmore, February 8th 2012

4 - 20. Inaction in RCMP harassment scandal should bother us all
By Gary Mason, Globe and Mail
Published Monday, Dec. 12, 2011

Chapter 5

A village where the leader isn't a bully!

As cited:

The PMO 'enemies list' is yet more evidence of the Stephen Harper government's tendency towards paranoia, secretiveness and bullying.[1]

At the risk of being added to the Harper government's recently discovered "enemies list," let's consider why the existence of such a document should give us all pause.[2]

Even former environment minister Peter Kent, a long-time Harper toady, was unsettled by the "juvenile" with-us-or-against-us frame . "That was the nomenclature used by [former U.S. president Richard] Nixon," he said. "His political horizon was divided very starkly into friends and enemies. The use of the word 'enemies list,' for those of us of a certain generation, it evokes nothing less than thoughts of Nixon and Watergate."[3]

The comparison to Nixon is unsettling. The disgraced former president was thought to view dissenters as adversaries to be destroyed rather than debated. The enemies list is just the latest piece of evidence that Prime Minister Stephen Harper has a tendency to think the same way.[4]

During a week in which Harper likely hoped for headlines about his government's reinvigorated, fresh-faced new cabinet, the shuffle was instead overshadowed by yet more evidence of some of the very political vulnerabilities it was meant to address : the government's paranoia, secretiveness and bullying. Those qualities have often served the government well politically. But the fact that Harper was unable to suppress them even when it would have been politically expedient to do so suggests just how deep-seated they are. [5]

As cited:

A fascio is a bunch or bundle. When applied to persons the word can best be translated as a band or gang.

Comparisons with the Nixon administration and Watergate are being raised following revelations the Harper government ordered "enemy" lists compiled in advance of this week's cabinet shuffle.[6]

Continuing:

The Prime Minister's Office sent an email to Conservative ministerial aides on July 4 asking to develop lists of troublesome bureaucrats as well as "friend and enemy stakeholders" for incoming ministers and their staff.[7]

The PMO has refused to comment on the controversy, which erupted after emails outlining the order were leaked to media outlets in Ottawa by an unidentified source on Monday, the same day as the federal cabinet shuffle.[8]

Reader's Comments:

Letter to the Editor posted July 9, 2013

Dear Editor, The benefit of doubt is exhausted in Stephen Harper's story that his former chief of staff acted alone when paying Mike Duffy's expense claims. It's a story that is simply unbelievable. The RCMP have confirmed three others in the PMO new of the schemes as well as the Conservative Party, which Stephen Harper is the leader of. But as of Saturday, July 6, 2013 Harper repeats the unbelievable. It reminds me of President Richard Nixon's statement, "I am not a crook."

No amount of cabinet shuffling by Stephen Harper, is going to deliver to Canada a better, responsible, progressive, honest government. It certainly won't disappear the Duffy / Wright scandal that surround Harper. A government that has the best interest of Canadians at heart is not what Harper and his comrades are all about.

CM
Parry Sound-Muskoa NDP Riding Association

Footnotes

1 – 5. Stephen Harper's 'enemies list' a reason to worry: Editorial, The Star, Opinion / Editorials, Published on Thu Jul 18 2013

6 – 8. Richard Nixon, Watergate cited as anger erupts over Stephen Harper government's 'enemy' list
By Lee Berthiaume, Postmedia News July 16, 2013

Chapter 6

A village where the leader doesn't control the law courts!

Why has our village leader appointed all of these Federal Court Judges:

Chief Justice Paul Crampton - Lawyer at Osler, Hoskin & Harcourt LLP
Russel Zinn - Lawyer at Ogilvy Renault LLP
Richard Boivin - Associate Senior Counsel with Aboriginal Affairs
Marie-Josée Bédard - Vice Chair of the Public Service Labour Board
André F.J. Scott - Chair of the Canadian International Trade Tribunal
Donald J. Rennie - Assistant Deputy Attorney General (Litigation)
Mary J.L. Gleason - Lawyer at Ogilvy Renault LLP
Jocelyne Gagné - Lawyer at Lavery, de Billy LLP
Catherine Kane - Department of Justice Senior General Counsel
Leonard S. Mandamin - Provincial Court of Alberta
Michael Manson - Lawyer at Smart & Biggar LLP
Yvan Roy - Deputy Secretary to the Cabinet
Cecily Strickland - Lawyer at Stewart McKelvey LLP
Peter Annis - Ontario Superior Court of Justice
Glennys L. McVeigh - Senior Counsel at Public Prosecutions

Apparently to solidify power?

No, our village leader wouldn't do that?

Let's look at this case:

Terry Mallenby took on some slimy bastards and won!

Staff Sgt John Thomas Randle was the original RCMP LIAR who said the husband was an unwilling witness at the 1976 Squamish, British Columbia, Canada inquest!

As can be seen in text, Terry Mallenby has the original Coroner Inquest report sent to him by the Coroner's office clearly indicating he was not an unwilling witness!!

In fact, the Coroner apologized to Terry Mallenby for listening to the Police lies that he was an "unwilling witness"!

Staff Sgt John Thomas Randle was the RCMP "arse hole" who wrote a letter in 1979 saying the husband was a murderer!

And to prove that Staff Sgt John Thomas Randle was not only a LIAR but a big, fat "arse hole" – Terry Mallenby used Randle's big fat lies to successfully sue the Queen of England, the Canada Government, the Royal Canadian Mounted Police and that "f--- up" RCMP Staff Sgt John Thomas Randle!!

Terry Mallenby also used RCMP John Thomas Randle's lies to be approved for a PTSD [Post-Tramatic Stress Disorder] pension, which he has received since he was age 28!

Why then did "Hitler" Harper and "shite head" Paulson upload these 40 year old RCMP lies to Sergey Brin's Google.ca and Google.com web sites??

What good is successfully suing in the Federal Court of Canada if the Canadian Prime Minister Stephen Harper ["Hitler" Harper] doesn't honor the Federal Court Judgment favor in Terry Mallenby's suit??

What good is successfully suing in the Federal Court of Canada if the RCMP Commissioner Robert Paulson doesn't honor the Federal Court Judgment favor in Terry Mallenby's suit??

Will any of these folks help Federal Court Chief Justice Paul Crampton to get Canadian Prime Minister to remove the 40 year old RCMP lies about Terry Mallenby from Sergey Brin's Google.ca and Google.com web sites?

This is doubly true when Canadian Prime Minister Stephen Harper flaunts the law and keeps these 40 year old RCMP lies about Terry Mallenby from Sergey Brin's Google.ca and Google.com web sites?

The Honourable Russel W. Zinn

Justice Zinn was born in Oxford County, Ontario.

He was educated at Carleton University (B.A. 1973 and M.A. (Philosophy) 1976) and the University of Ottawa (LL.B. 1979).

Following his call to the Ontario Bar in 1981, he became an Associate and later a Partner with Gowling & Henderson in Ottawa (1981-1993).

He joined Ogilvy Renault LLP as a Partner and in 2006 was appointed a Senior Partner (2001-2008).

Justice Zinn's legal practice focused on human rights, labour and employment, access and privacy law issues.

He is the author of The Law of Human Rights in Canada: Practice and Procedure (Canada Law Book, 1996).

The Honourable Richard Boivin

Born in 1964 in Montréal, Québec.

Educated at Collège de Montréal, Université de Montréal Min. Hist. (1985), University of Ottawa LL.L. (1988), B.A. (1990), LL.M. (1995) and University of London LL.M. (1991) (King's College).

The Honourable Marie-Josée Bédard

Born in Montreal, Justice Bédard studied at the University of Ottawa where she obtained a bachelor's degree in administration in 1989 and a degree in civil law in 1992.

She practiced with the firm Bédard, Saucier in employment law, administrative law and municipal law.

The Honourable André F.J. Scott

Born in Ottawa, Ontario. Education at the University of Ottawa: BA (1972), LL.L (1975), LL.M. (1980) in business law.

Lecturer at the Faculty of civil law of the University of Ottawa.

The Honourable Donald J. Rennie

Mr. Justice Rennie received a Bachelor of Arts (B.A.) from the University of Guelph in 1975 and a Bachelor of Laws (LL.B.) from Dalhousie University in 1978.

Over the course of his 29 years of practice he appeared as counsel for the Attorney General of Canada in many complex cases involving the Charter of Rights and Freedoms, administrative, tort and constitutional law.

He is the author of numerous legal articles, most recently "Application of the Charter of Rights" in the 2009 Supreme Court Law Review.

The Honourable Mary J.L. Gleason

Justice Gleason was born in Regina, Saskatchewan.

She obtained a B.A.(Honours) in History from the University of Ottawa in 1981 and an Bachelor of Laws (LL.B.) from Dalhousie University in 1984.

She was a senior partner with Norton Rose, LLP (formerly Ogilvy Renault, LLP) and practiced labour and employment law in Ottawa with that firm for nearly 26 years.

She was a founding member of CACE, its first (and to date only) female President [the Canadian Association of Counsel to Employers].

The Honourable Jocelyne Gagné

Born in Kingston, Ontario.

He studied economics at the University of Quebec at Montréal and in 1989 received a Bachelor of Laws from the University of Montréal.

She practised civil and commercial litigation with Desjardins Ducharme until joining Lavery, deBilly in 2007.

The Honourable Catherine M. Kane

Born in Ottawa, Ontario.

Educated at Saint Patrick's College (BA 1977) and the University of Ottawa (LLB 1980).

The Honourable Leonard S. Mandamin

Born in 1944, an Anishnawbe member of the Wikwemikong Unceded Indian Reserve on Manitoulin Island, Ontario.

Educated at University of Waterloo (B.A.Sc. - Electrical Engineering 1971), University of Alberta (LL.B. 1982).

Faculty Co-ordinator for Aboriginal Justice Seminars at the Banff School of Management and Adjunct Professor at the University of Alberta School of Native Studies.

President of the Canadian Native Friendship Centre in Edmonton, Alberta (1990).

The Honourable Michael D. Manson

Born February 17, 1955, in Vancouver, British Columbia.

Educated at McGill University (BSc. 1976; Dip.Ed. 1978) and University of British Columbia (L.L.B. 1982).

Associate and Partner at Smart & Biggar (1984-2012); Adjunct Professor of the University of Victoria (1996-2012).

The Honourable Glennys L. McVeigh

She attended the University of Saskatchewan, College of Arts, and completed a bachelor of laws in 1992.

From 1992 to 1998, she was an associate with Jamieson Bains in Saskatoon, where she practised in civil and criminal litigation.

She was a part-time lecturer at the University of Saskatchewan Law School from 2009 to 2010.

What will these Federal Court Judges do about these illegal acts by Canadian Prime Minister Stephen Harper?

What will these Federal Court Judges do about these illegal acts by RCMP Commissioner Robert Paulson?

Nothing as usual because they are in Canadian Prime Minister Stephen Harper's "back-pocket" since he appointed all of them??

Chapter 7

It's a village where the leader in waiting is honest and ethical!

A village where the leader in waiting doesn't bilk a senior charity out of $20,000?

Our village leader in waiting appears to be Justin Trudeau?

Justin Trudeau has a Bachelor of Arts degree from McGill University, and A Bachelor of Education degree from the University of British Columbia.

He was born on December 25, 1971, the eldest son of the late former Prime Minister Pierre Elliott Trudeau and Margaret Sinclair Trudeau Kemper.

Terry Mallenby has a BSW from McGill University and a BA, and MA from Simon Fraser University in British Columbia.

Justin Trudeau says we need a new leadership for Canada!

Justin Trudeau says "I love this country and I want to serve it. I am Running because I believe Canada wants and needs new leadership.

The Conservative government is taking this country in a direction most Canadians don't want it to go.

We need a vision for our future grounded not in the politics of envy or mistrust!"

Justin Trudeau says "in the coming months, I will be traveling the country Talking with Canadians about the challenges, concerns and issues that affect us all.

As part of this process, I intend to share my views about what I'm hearing and how I think we can overcome these challenges together.

I hope to generate positive, open and constructive debate.

How would Justin Trudeau like to answer as the new Prime Minister of Canada, what will you do about these illegal acts by Canadian Prime Minister Stephen Harper and RCMP Commissioner Robert Paulson – in your positive, open and constructive run for   government?

As cited:

"Justin Trudeau repays expenses claimed for private trips"
By Leslie MacKinnon, CBC News Posted: Jan 16, 2014

Liberal Leader Justin Trudeau admitted Thursday he claimed
expenses for private speaking engagements, saying the
claims were an error and he has repaid them. (Adrain
Wylde/Canadian Press)

Hello Trudeau, you can't tell the difference between our money (taxpayer's money) and
your money??

And then you lie about it?

*NDP Leader Tom Mulcair, speaking to reporters outside the NDP caucus room in the
House of Commons, pointed out that in June Trudeau had denied spending parliamentary
resources while conducting his speaking engagements.*

*"Frankly, I think he's stolen a page from Stephen Harper's playbook — deny, deny, deny
— until you get caught and then you apologize," Mulcair said.*

And, according to Glen McGregor, Justin Trudeau admits that he 'won the lottery' with
$1.2 million inheritance!

So, Justin Trudeau is a millionaire and he can't apparently tell the difference between
your money as a tax payer and the million dollars he has squirreled away??

*Liberal Leader Justin Trudeau has disclosed that he wrongly claimed $840 in expenses
that were unrelated to his duties as an MP.*

Makes you wonder about the guy?

What's going to happen when he becomes Prime Minister and he has unlimited access to your money??

As cited by Doug Hempstead in the Ottawa Sun:

Former Ottawa police chief Senator Vern White says people shouldn't brag about breaking the law.

That's his perception of comments this week by federal Liberal leader, Justin Trudeau.

"It is immature for him to be bragging — and that's what I think he is doing — about breaking a criminal law," White said, via Skype.

Trudeau admitted to having taken a puff off a joint, while at a barbecue.

At the time, he was already an elected MP.

White said that distinction is significant.

"If he had been talking about mistakes, or even something he had done previous to his being elected to Canadian parliament, then I would see this as an error in judgment but this is something else," said White.

"What a terrible message to send to our youth. He is the leader of the Liberal party and an elected representative and I expect more from those who serve this country in this capacity."

As further cited:

"Justin Trudeau admits smoking marijuana as MP"
By Joanna Smith, Ottawa Bureau reporter, Published on Thu Aug 22 2013

"We had a few good friends over for a dinner party, our kids were at their grandmother's for the night, and one of our friends lit a joint and passed it around. I had a puff," Trudeau said.

His political rivals disagreed.

"By flouting the laws of Canada while holding elected office, he shows he is a poor example for all Canadians, particularly young ones. Justin Trudeau is simply not the kind of leader our country needs," Justice Minister Peter MacKay said in a statement Thursday.

Reader's Comment:

After Justin Trudeau admits smoking marijuana as an MP, Peter MacKay quickly and publicly denounces him. This is interesting coming from a minister who used a military helicopter as his personal taxi at a cost of $32,000 to taxpayers.

This is the same minister who, while working on the F-35 project, put the decimal in the wrong place at a cost of $10 billion.

Trudeau's judgment may have been clouded by smoking pot. What's MacKay's excuse?

JOHN ALKSNIS
Winnipeg

However Dave Breakenridge of the Calgary Sun, apparently gave an account of Justin Trudeau as being a "two-faced" freak in his article entitled "Justin Trudeau, police chiefs offering hypocrisy and half-measures on pot"!

Justin Trudeau recently came out in favour of legalization of marijuana in this country, then went further, saying he has smoked weed while an MP.

But I hope those who were fawning over his admission actually take a look at his public record on pot.

He has been cool to legalization, according to a recent editorial: "He has said legalization would likely increase marijuana consumption, which is 'not great for your health' and 'disconnects you a little bit from the world,' adding, 'I don't know that it's entirely consistent with the kind of society we're trying to build.'"

In 2010, he even spoke out against decriminalization: "I lived in Whistler for years and have seen the effects," Trudeau told Maclean's. "We need all our brain cells to deal with our problems."

And here's more about Justin Trudeau!

As cited:

"Justin Trudeau defends poor Commons attendance record"
Lee Berthiaume, Postmedia News, December 10, 2013

Liberal Leader Justin Trudeau is making no apologies for appearing in the House of Commons only two days per week during this fall's session of Parliament.

Wow, I'm sure other hard working people would enjoy a job where you can skip out three days of the work week – each and every week like Justin Trudeau apparently does??

And here's more about Justin Trudeau!

"Trudeau admits he was wrong charging charity $20,000 for speech"
June 16, 2013 — BC Blue

Liberal leader Justin Trudeau tried his best to keep the unethical cash that a seniors charity had asked for back after he proved to be a fund-raising bust!

Trudeau went on CTV today trying to justify his immoral behaviour by lamely calling himself a professional "environmental educational advocate"?

Between 2006 and 2009, he made $1.3 million through the speaking events — more than the value of the stocks and bonds he inherited from his father.

What is this Millionaire "arse hole"charging these benevolent organizations fees?

Here's a partial list of his exorbitant fees:

May 3, 2006 – Elementary Teachers Federation of Ontario. $10,000

May 10, 2006 – Professional Administrators of Volunteer Resoucres. $7,500

May 10, 2006 – Toronto District School Board. $5,000

May 12, 2006 – Toronto School Administrators Association. $7,500

May 13, 2006 – The Learning Partnership. $10,000

June 7, 2006 – Ontario Association of Children's Aid Societies c, 20o Meeting Management Services. $7,500

August 23, 2006 – Incentive Works. $7,500

September 30, 2006 – Waterloo Region District School Board. $7,500

October 14, 2006 – Nova Scotia Nature Trust. $7,500

October 20, 2006 – Canadian Parks & Recreation Association. $10,000

October 26, 2006 – Ministry of Children & Youth Services. $8,000

November 7, 2006 – Ontario Hospital Association. $10,000

November 17, 2006 – Alberta Teachers' Association. $7,500

November 21, 2006 – Canadian Water Network. $9,000

December 6, 2006 – Ministry of Community & Social Services. $7,500

January 24, 2007 – University of Manitoba – Student's Union. $10,000

February 9, 2007 – Ottawa Carlton District School Board. $10,000

February 16, 2007 – Reading for the Love of it. $7,500

March 15, 2007 – Alberta Teachers' Association. $10,000

April 3, 2007 – Rapport Youth & Family Services. $10,000

May 4, 2007 – New Brunswick Teachers' Association. $10,000

May 5, 2007 – South Huron District Secondary School Council. $10,000

May 8, 2007 – Community Safety & Crime Prevention Council of Waterloo. $10,000

May 13, 2007 – Blessed Events. $10,000

May 14, 2007 – Canadian Association of Healthcare Philanthropy. $10,000

May 17 & 18, 2007 – Niagara Catholic District School Board. $15,000

June 5, 2007 – London Interfaith Counselling Centre. $10,000

August 21, 2007 – First Nations Water Conference – Smith's Landing First Nation . $6,000

September 7, 2007 – Human Concern International. $10,000

September 24, 2007 – Sudbury & District Health Unit. $10,000

November 18, 2007 – Canadian Tamil Youth Development Centre. $10,000

November 18, 2007 – National Council of Jewish Women of Canada. $10,000

January 25, 2008 – Ontario Camping Association. $10,000

March 28, 2008 – Charity of Hope. $10,000

April 9, 2008 – Youth Environmental Network of York Region. $10,000

May 6, 2008 – Canadian Mental Health Association – Grey Bruce Branch. $15,000

May 9, 2008 – Children of Hope. $10,000

June 13, 2008 – Community Living Ontario. $10,000

October 20, 2008 – London Health Sciences Centre. $10,000

January 31, 2009 – Ontario Library Association. $10,000

November 2, 2009 – The Learning Partnership. $10,000

November 6, 2009 – Waterloo Catholic District School Board. $15,000

April 23, 2010 – Charity of Hope. $15,000

May 7, 2010 – Algonquin & Lakeshore Catholic District School Board. $15,000

June 9, 2011 – Kincardine District Secondary School, Kincardine, ON. $10,000

April 30, 2012 – Literacy for Life, Saskatoon, SK. $20,000

June 26, 2012 – Canadian Mental Health Association – Halton Region, Burlington, ON. $20,000

Conservative MP Rob Moore reacts:

"I have always believed that Justin Trudeau's practice of charging tens of thousands of dollars to charities, churches and seniors groups was not right and went against the understood practice of our duties as Members of Parliament," Moore said.

NDP MP Charlie Angus reacts:

NDP MP Charlie Angus on Thursday questioned why a sitting MP would need to charge Canadians to hear him speak.

"I'm not Justin Trudeau but I consider that part of my parliamentary work, so I wouldn't charge that because I'm paid for, paid by the taxpayer," Angus told reporters after question period.

Readers react:

Sean M Says:
June 16, 2013 at 4:39 PM
When Trudumb is PM… ??? LOL… thats a funny one! The idiot hasn't done anything in his life for more than 2 years, so I guess he better win in 2015, which i seriously doubt.

Anne in swON Says:
June 16, 2013 at 5:51 PM
The point of the whole thing is that as an MP he should not have been charging a speaker's fee to charities. That's where the optics are bad.

Then again, how can anyone expect Justin Trudeau to do the right thing and get Canadian Prime Minister Stephen Harper to remove the illegal 40 year old RCMP lies about Terry Mallenby from Sergey Brin's Google.ca and Google.com web sites?

Then again, as reported by Michael Harris, Canadian Prime Minister Stephen Harper is no better – he uses your tax payer dollars to promote himself!

This time it's Stephen Harper helping himself to public dollars in a truly offensive fashion.

The scam is as simple as it is brazen: Harper has spent hundreds of millions of taxpayers' dollars promoting his government. Often, it's the highly partisan stuff that should be paid for by the Conservative party. He's using public money for political gain — and doing it in a time of cutbacks.

When Harper first started promoting his government with public money, ministers like Rona Ambrose were trotted out to say that the justification for showering ad agencies with tax dollars was the task of "informing" Canadians about government services and programs.

In other words, not only was it a freeloading political announcement paid for by Canadians on behalf of the Conservative party, it was false.

Chapter 8

A village where the leader doesn't suppress the truth!

The Village Police do everything they can to railroad Terry Mallenby into jail!!

Let's put this part of the story into perspective as a very apparent RCMP [Royal Canadian Mounted Police] and Canadian Government Conspiracy:

1976   Coroner's Inquest held in Squamish, British Columbia, Canada ruled the homicide was by Person or Persons Unknown

That "dirt-bag" RCMP S/Sgt John Thomas Randle lies at the 1976 Coroner's Inquest held in Squamish, British Columbia, Canada falsely stating the husband was an unwilling witness so the RCMP could arrest him?

The only problem is that because of this "arse hole's" lies, the husband missed his wife's funeral!!

You can imagine the anguish this caused the husband!!

And to prove that RCMP Staff Sgt John Thomas Randle is a big, fat liar and a "bloody arse hole" – Terry Mallenby used Randle's big fat lies to successfully sue the Queen of England, the Canada Government and the Royal Canadian Mounted Police including RCMP Staff Sgt John Thomas Randle!!

1976   Coroner's Inquest held in Squamish, British Columbia, Canada ruled the homicide was by Person or Persons Unknown

The Coroner apologized to Terry Mallenby for listening to the RCMP that he was an "unwilling witness"!

Because of the RCMP lies, Terry Mallenby missed his wife's funeral!

Terry Mallenby will hate the RCMP until the day he dies!

And Terry Mallenby will have books written about the RCMP scum to show the kind of "shit" they pull on the "little people"

And this book is just one in a series that tells the bitter truth about the RCMP!

It also tells how Canadian Prime Minister Stephen Harper has had these 40 year old RCMP lies uploaded to Sergey Brin's Google.ca and Google web site!

Why did Canadian Prime Minister Stephen Harper do that unethical thing, as payback to Terry Mallenby because he successfully sued the Royal Canadian Mounted Police over their lies – receiving a $275,000 out of court settlement!

Canadian Prime Minister Stephen Harper is so unethical – he doesn't care and uploads these 40 year old RCMP lies anyway!!

And Sergey Brin is another useless Billionaire with no scruples; he doesn't remove these 40 year old RCMP lies from his Google.ca and Google web site!

1979	Terry Mallenby was offered a Social Work job in Scotland, but to make sure Terry Mallenby never worked again – The RCMP wrote a letter in 1979 and spread it around the world!
1979	Not satisfied with his lies in 1976, RCMP S/Sgt John Thomas Randle writes a letter saying that the husband was a murderer[1]
1979	RCMP S/Sgt John Thomas Randle writes a letter saying that Terry Mallenby was a murderer to make sure he remained unemployed[1]
1979	RCMP S/Sgt John Thomas Randle writes a letter saying that Terry Mallenby was a murderer is given to John Gomery to make sure Terry Mallenby remained unemployed[2a]
1979	M.J. Hauser of the Correctional Service of Canada in memo(s) also says that Terry Mallenby was a murderer to make sure he remained unemployed[3]
1979	Nicole Bomberg of the Canadian Human Rights Commission in memo(s) also says that Terry Mallenby was a murderer to make sure he remained unemployed[4]
1979	Lorisa Stein of the Canadian Human Rights Commission in memo(s) also says that Terry Mallenby was a murderer to make sure he remained unemployed[5]
1980	Terry Mallenby being unemployed seeks relief from his Canada Student Loans, however, the Judge turns out to be John Gomery and his request is denied[2b]

1980	Terry Mallenby being unemployed seeks a disability pension [Canada Pension Plan] using RCMP S/Sgt John Thomas Randle, M.J. Hauser of the Correctional Service of Canada memo(s), Nicole Bomberg of the Canadian Human Rights Commission memo(s) and Lorisa Stein of the Canadian Human Rights Commission memo(s) – his request for disability pension approved
1981	Terry Mallenby being unemployed again seeks relief from his Canada Student Loans, the Judge not being John Gomery, and his request is approved
1981	The RCMP fabricate more "bull shit" about Terry Mallenby to railroad him into jail
1990	After 14 years of accumulating evidence, Terry successfully sues the RCMP over their lies [see Appendix 1, cited below]
1990	Terry Mallenby was hired by the Newfoundland Social Services Department as a Social Worker.
1993	However, Terry Mallenby would not cover-up the lax security at the Whitbourne Centre run by Newfoundland Social Service Minister Kay Young [see Appendix 2, cited below]

Terry Mallenby blew the whistle on the lax security at the Whitbourne Centre run by Newfoundland Social Service Minister Kay Young.

Newfoundland Social Service Minister Kay Young and Newfoundland Premier Clyde Wells fabricated some bull-shit about Terry Mallenby to get rid of him for blowing the whistle on the lax security at the Whitbourne Centre!

Because they ignored Terry Mallenby's warning, deaths occurred at the Whitbourne Centre!

The Canadian unemployment department could see that Terry Mallenby had done nothing wrong for blowing the whistle on the lax security at the Whitbourne Centre and approved his application for unemployment benfits!

1995	Terry Mallenby was offered a Social Work job in Alberta.

However, Premier Ralph Klein made sure Terry Mallenby did

not take up this position.

Was it a favor to Newfoundland Premier Clyde Wells to keep Terry Mallenby unemployed?

Was it a favor to the Royal Canadian Mounted Police to keep Terry Mallenby unemployed?

1996   Being unemployed, Terry Mallenby went back on his Canada Pension Plan disability pension with a psychiatrist diagnosis that he suffered with Post Traumatic Stress – Chronic Type, Social Phobia, etc [see Appendix 3, cited below]

1990   As part of dealing with his Post Traumatic Stress – Chronic Type Terry Mallenby took to writing about the RCMP false statements, harassment, illegal, acts:

> *Human rights violations in Canada: Individual being denied employment with the Federal Government of Canada due to false "murder charge" statements made by M.J. Hauser of the Correctional Service of Canada (continuing case study from Cour supérieure en matière de faillite, Palais de justice, Montréal, File #500-11-002290-894)OCLC Number: 29205400 – 1990*

> *Human rights violations in Canada: Individual being denied employment with the Federal Government of Canada due to false "murder charge" statements made by Nicole Bomberg of the Public Service Commission of Canada (continuing case study from Cour supérieure en matière de faillite, Palais de justice, Montréal, File #500-11-002290-894)OCLC Number: 29205400 – 1990*

1996   As part of dealing with his Post Traumatic Stress – Chronic Type Terry Mallenby took to writing about the RCMP false statements, harassment, illegal, acts:

> *R.C.M.P. Sgt. John ("Jack") Thomas Randle's legacy to Canada. ISBN: 0969594429 9780969594420 OCLC Number: 46531882 - 1996*

> *R.C.M.P. Sgt. John ("Jack") Thomas Randle's legacy to Canada. ISBN: 0969594429 9780969594420 OCLC Number: 46531882 - 1996*

1997   As part of dealing with his Post Traumatic Stress – Chronic

Type Terry Mallenby took to writing about the RCMP false statements, harassment, illegal, acts:

> *Human rights violations in Canada by federal agents of the Canadian Human Rights Anti-Discrimination Agency of the Public Service Commission of Canada.*
> *ISBN: 0969594453 9780969594451*
> *OCLC Number: 46528081 - 1997*

> *Is he Canada's example of another Mark Furman : R.C.M.P. Sgt. John ("Jack") Thomas Randle purposefully committed lies, fabricated evidence, made false statements & committed illegal acts! ISBN: 0969594437 9780969594437*
> *OCLC Number: 43152171 - 1997*

> *Complete discharge from bankruptcy including preferred student loans due to Royal Canadian Mounted Police harassment: a most unusual case of bankruptcy.*
> *ISBN: 0968290469 9780968290460*
> *OCLC Number: 46563182 – 1997*

1998   As part of dealing with his Post Traumatic Stress – Chronic Type Terry Mallenby took to writing about the RCMP false statements, harassment, illegal, acts:

> *Canadian anti-discriminate [sic] directorate and Canadian public service staff Nicole Bomberg's legacy to Canada.*
> *ISBN: 0968290469 9780968290460*
> *OCLC Number: 46563169 - 1998*

> *Canadian anti-discrimination directorate and Canadian public service staff Lorisa Stein's legacy to Canada.*
> *N: 096959447X 9780969594475*
> *OCLC Number: 46563137 - 1998*

> *Royal Canadian Mounted Police officers Sgt. John ("Jack") Thomas Randle's & Cpl. Jackett's legacy to Canada.*
> *ISBN: 0968290442 9780968290446*
> *OCLC Number: 46563215 - 1998*

> *Judge John Gomery's inapproprivate comments based on lies, false statements, fabricated statements & illegal acts by R.C.M.P. Sgt. John Thomas Randle.*
> *ISBN: 0968290477 9780968290477*
> *OCLC Number: 46563154 – 1998*

Can police harassment involving illegal acts, false statements and fabricated evidence lead to a diagnosis of post-traumatic stress disorder sufficient to approve permanent disability pension? ISBN: 0969594488 9780969594482 OCLC Number: 46563102 - 1998

1998   The United Nations wasn't interested in Terry Mallenby:

Kofi Annan, Secretary General of the United Nations and Mary Robinson, the Human Rights Commissioner: their legacy to the world. OCLC Number: 49268248

1998   To shut the Terry Mallenby up, the RCMP fabricate more "bull shit" about Terry Mallenby in another attempt to railroad him into jail

2000   The Canadian Investigative Program wasn't interested in Terry Mallenby:

Story 'too hot' for the investigative program "The Fifth Estate"!! OCLC Number: 48670944

2005   How dare Terry Mallenby move his family back to British Columbia, Canada – the RCMP would surely make his life miserable, including his wife and children!

Did apparent RCMP stooge professor Helen Brown purposefully fabricate a statement about Terry Mallenby's son to interfere with his university program[6]

This RCMP stooge professor Helen Brown also tried the same with Terry Mallenby's daughter

2006   Did the RCMP have the Canadian Military purposefully issue Terry Mallenby's daughter clown sized boots so she would not make BMQ and eliminate her from a career with the Canadian military [7]

2007   Did the RCMP have the Canadian Military apparently "poison" Terry Mallenby's son so he would not make BMQ and eliminate him from a career with the Canadian military[8]

2008   The RCMP had some ruffians harass Terry Mallenby's wife, daughter and son[9]

2009   Terry Mallenby moved his family to Winnipeg, Manitoba, Canada to get away fom the RCMP harassment in British

Columbia, Canada!

Did the RCMP have a private security employer in Winnipeg, Manitoba, Canada deny Terry Mallenby's son essential emails[10]

2009   Did RCMP stooge Canadian Minister Diane Finley purposefully accept lies of a private security employer about Terry Mallenby's son and daughter to eliminate a career in private security[11]

2010   The RCMP made up some cock-and-bull reason not to accept Terry Mallenby's son as a recruit thus eliminating his potential career with the RCMP[12]

The RCMP said Terry Mallenby's son had two university degrees and so he was unsuitable?

The RCMP said Terry Mallenby's son liked to "catch bad guys" so he was unsuitable?

The RCMP said Terry Mallenby's son lived at home so he was unsuitable?

Let's look a little closer at this RCMP 'bull-shite' about Terry Mallenby's son?

Instead of hiring a clean-cut recruit like Terry Mallenby's son, the idiot, dumb shite RCMP incredible as it sounds have gone to hiring drug convicted individuals?

The RCMP, which is on a hiring blitz, will now turn a blind eye to some indiscretions by its applicants, including some drug activities, CBC News has learned.

An internal memo obtained by CBC News reveals the RCMP has changed its policy on drug use "to permit consideration of mitigating factors in all cases of criminal activity, which may include drug trafficking, etc."

What to "f---", instead of hiring Terry Mallenby's clean-cut son, the dumb shite RCMP have gone to hiring drug traffickers????

Does anyone think this is the stupidest thing they have ever heard?

Well the reaction to this ridiculous idea came out good and strong in the "Story Comments" section:

This is such a joke! You can't have criminals being police officers! What are these people on?

I thought the RCMP already hired from the bottom of the barrel? What is left?

Sure, relax the rules and give each new officer 2 tasers. Then they can be twice as dangerous to the public.

I think the standards are too low now. Look at the four liars from Vancouver.

I cannot see how 'lowering the standards' to help in qualifying more candidates for the RCMP is' a step in the right direction'. We should be seeking better quality people for the force, reliable people with a clean background not folks who have committed indiscretions, minor or otherwise. RCMP Officers carry guns, tasers etc. and have a great responsibility to society. We need the very best candidates possible.

RCMP still had some credibility they could find credible applicants. I certainly don't paint all officers with the same brush but the actions of some officers, and how those actions were handled by the institution, have really damaged perceptions of the RCMP. Before looking at lower standards for applicants they should look at higher standards for themselves.

2010	Did RCMP stooge Manitoba Health Minister Theresa Oswald purposefully accept lies from the "cool kids gang" to harass, isolate and discriminate against Terry Mallenby's daughter[13]
	Did RCMP stooge Manitoba Health Minister Theresa Oswald's "cool kids gang" also try to harass and isolate Terry Mallenby's son
2011	The Canadian Government and RCMP are censoring this current author's attempts to bring this conspiracy to light, where the Canadian Government and the RCMP are obviously censoring what appears on Amazon.com[14]
2012	Canadian Prime Minister Stephen Harper and RCMP

Commissioner Robert Paulson upload their 1976 RCMP lies to Sergey Brin's Google and Google.ca internet web site as more harassment and to make sure Terry Mallenby, his wife and children also remain unemployed!!

2013   Senator Larry W. Campbell, former RCMP officer, and former Chief Coroner says he doesn't give a "shite" about the 1976 Coroner Inquest results – the RCMP will continue their campaign of illegal acts, harassment of Terry Mallenby, his wife, and children!!

After all, the RCMP are above the law!!

And they can do as they please, especially with Canadian Prime Minister Stephen Harper at the helm!!

And that unethical RCMP Commissioner Robert Paulson who still denies female RCMP officers have been sexually harassed for decades!!

The RCMP and the Canadian Government still owe this "little guy" one million dollars in lost wages, when is he going to receive it?

Footnotes

1. The Terry Mallenby knew full-well long, long ago that there were "lying bastards" in the RCMP [interspersed amongst the many fine RCMP officers protecting our citizens and country]!

BOOK SUPPRESSED BY "HITLER" HARPER!
Canada's Police Force: Lies, fabrication, perjury ... and much worse?
"Before his death he was able to tell a nurse at the hospital that an RCMP officer jumped up and down on him"

2a & 2b. The Terry Mallenby knew full-well long, long ago what a "miserable bastard" John Gomery was and has waited over 30 years before the rest of the country and world would find out about him:

BOOK SUPPRESSED BY "HITLER" HARPER!
A Federal Court ruling has blasted the biased musings of Judge John Gomery

3 - 5. The Terry Mallenby knew full-well long, long ago what "lying bastards" were employed by the Federal Government of Canada and has waited over 30 years before the rest of the country and world would find out about such things:

BOOK SUPPRESSED BY "HITLER" HARPER!
There's No Such Thing as Human Rights in Canada!

6. The Terry Mallenby knew full-well long, long ago what "lying bastards" were employed by the Federal Government of Canada and the RCMP and here is the story about the "lying professor" as an apparent RCMP stooge who tried to interfere with the Terry Mallenby son's education:

BOOK SUPPRESSED BY "HITLER" HARPER!
The lying professor? And, the lying V.P.?

7. The Terry Mallenby knew full-well long, long ago what "lying bastards" were employed by the Federal Government of Canada and the RCMP and here is the story about the "lying doctor" as an apparent RCMP stooge who tried to interfere with the Terry Mallenby daughter's potential military career:

BOOK SUPPRESSED BY "HITLER" HARPER!
The lying doctor? And, the lying general?

8. The Terry Mallenby knew full-well long, long ago what "lying bastards" were employed by the Federal Government of Canada and the RCMP and here is the story about the apparent attempted "poisoning" of the Terry Mallenby son's thus eliminating his potential military career:

BOOK SUPPRESSED BY "HITLER" HARPER!
Canadian Government Conspiracy: Was this 'kid' poisoned?

9. The Terry Mallenby knew full-well long, long ago what "lying bastards" were employed by the Federal Government of Canada and the RCMP and here is the story about the harassment of the "little guy's" wife and daughter and son by RCMP stooges:

Canada's Police Force: Lies, fabrication, perjury ... and much worse?
"Before his death he was able to tell a nurse at the hospital that an RCMP officer jumped up and down on him"

10. The Terry Mallenby knew full-well long, long ago what "lying bastards" were employed by the Federal Government of Canada and the RCMP and here is the story about a vindictive employer as an apparent RCMP stooge who tried to interfere with the Terry Mallenby son's safety:

BOOK SUPPRESSED BY "HITLER" HARPER!
Canada's Very Own "Three Blind Mice"! Who concluded that antibiotics are for stress?

11. The Terry Mallenby knew full-well long, long ago what "lying bastards" were employed by the Federal Government of Canada and the RCMP and here is the story about a vindictive employer as an apparent RCMP stooge who tried to interfere with the Terry Mallenby daughter's employment:

BOOK SUPPRESSED BY "HITLER" HARPER!
Vindictive Employers: Nothing but poison!

12. The Terry Mallenby knew full-well long, long ago what "lying bastards" were employed by the Federal Government of Canada and the RCMP and here is the story about the RCMP making up some cock-and-bull nonsense so they would not have to accept the "little guy's" son as an RCMP recruit:

BOOK SUPPRESSED BY "HITLER" HARPER!
If You Like To Catch Bad Guys This Police Force Doesn't Want You?

13. The Terry Mallenby knew full-well long, long ago what "lying bastards" were employed by the Federal Government of Canada and the RCMP and here is the story about the RCMP using a provincial government department to sex-discriminate, harass, and isolate the "little guy's" daughter:

BOOK SUPPRESSED BY "HITLER" HARPER!
Is slavery alive and well in Canada? There is absolutely no protection for female employees against vindictive employers!

14. The Canadian Government and RCMP are censoring this current author's attempts to bring this conspiracy against this Terry Mallenby and his family to light, where the Canadian Government and the RCMP are obviously censoring what appears on Amazon.com:

BOOK SUPPRESSED BY "HITLER" HARPER!
Is Canada's Police Force Filtering What the World Reads about Them? The "Crazy Canuck" apparently wrote a bogus review to help out?

As noted, Lorisa Stein one of the Canadian Human Rights staff wrote a false memo in 1979 that Terry Mallenby was a murderer to make sure he remained unemployed - Lorisa Stein also graduated from Queen's University in Kingston, Ontario, Canada.

What kind of people does Queen's University in Kingston, Ontario, Canada produce??

Possibly liars and skunks like Lorisa Stein??

Is this the same Lorisa Stein?

If yes, then Lorisa Stein classes herself as:

Lorisa Stein, Family Law Lawyer
150 York Street, Suite 800
 Toronto,Ontario
MSH 3S5
Fax: (416) 596-0599
Phone: 416 596- 8081

I attended Queen's University for my law degree, Carleton University and University of Toronto for my Master's degree in Political Sciences (Public Policy), and Western University and Universidad Iberoamericana for my Honours BA. Earning three degrees attending seven universities in five cities over 15 years shows my commitment, determination and dedication to following my dreams.

I am a member of the Law Society of Upper Canada, the Board of Directors of Collaborative Practice Toronto, the Association of Family and Conciliation Courts (AFCC), and the International Academy of Collaborative Practitioners (IACP).

Appendix 1a

Terry Mallenby sued for lost wages of 1.3 million dollars [with actuarial evidence] and the first out-of-court settlement that the Federal Government of Canada and the RCMP offered him was $150,000?

The Terry Mallenby told the lawyer that wasn't enough, and the second out-of-court settlement that the Federal Government of Canada and the RCMP offered him was $275,000?

The Terry Mallenby said that represented a moral victory over "the bastards" and said accept it!

As far as the Terry Mallenby is concerned, the Federal Government of Canada and the RCMP still owe him the remaining 1 million dollars, together with a sizeable amount for his wife and children who have themselves been harassed by the Federal Government of Canada and the RCMP!

As for the current author can tell, all he can say is that there are apparently many "lying shit-heads" working for the Federal Government of Canada and the RCMP and that there is enough material out there in the press about them:

Perverts, Sexual Deviants Occupy Top RCMP Ranks – New Allegations Suggest
Saturday, November 12th, 2011
The Link Paper

Appendix 1b The Terry Mallenby successfully sued RCMP!

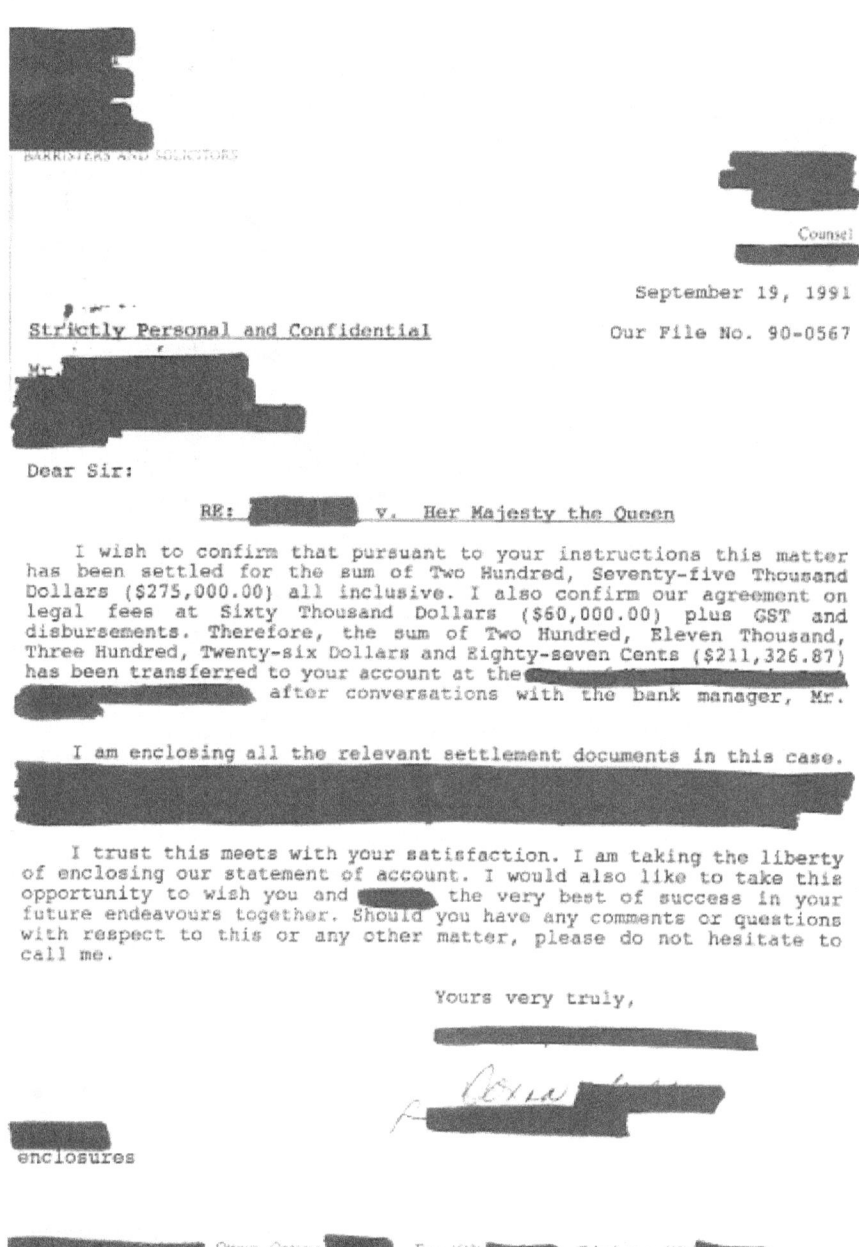

BARRISTERS AND SOLICITORS

Counsel

September 19, 1991

<u>Strictly Personal and Confidential</u>   Our File No. 90-0567

Mr.

Dear Sir:

<u>RE: v.   Her Majesty the Queen</u>

I wish to confirm that pursuant to your instructions this matter
has been settled for the sum of Two Hundred, Seventy-five Thousand
Dollars ($275,000.00) all inclusive. I also confirm our agreement on
legal fees at Sixty Thousand Dollars ($60,000.00) plus GST and
disbursements. Therefore, the sum of Two Hundred, Eleven Thousand,
Three Hundred, Twenty-six Dollars and Eighty-seven Cents ($211,326.87)
has been transferred to your account at the
                         after conversations with the bank manager, Mr.

I am enclosing all the relevant settlement documents in this case.

I trust this meets with your satisfaction. I am taking the liberty
of enclosing our statement of account. I would also like to take this
opportunity to wish you and   the very best of success in your
future endeavours together. Should you have any comments or questions
with respect to this or any other matter, please do not hesitate to
call me.

Yours very truly,

enclosures

Ottawa, Ontario   Fax (613)   Telephone (613)

52

Appendix 1c The Terry Mallenby successfully sued RCMP!

No: T-1131 93

IN THE FEDERAL COURT OF CANADA
TRIAL DIVISION

BETWEEN:

▒▒▒▒▒▒▒ ,

and

Plaintiffs

AND:

HER MAJESTY THE QUEEN, ROYAL CANADIAN
MOUNTED POLICE and J.I. RANDLE.

Defendants

DECLARATION OF SETTLEMENT

The parties, by their counsel, hereby declare that the
present case has now been settled, each party paying its own costs.

SIGNED in Montreal, this ____
day of September 1991

Appendix 1d The Terry Mallenby successfully sued RCMP!

Minister of Justice
and Attorney General of Canada

Ministre de la Justice
et Procureur général du Canada

A. Kim Campbell, P.C., Q.C., M.P./o.p., c.r., députée

OCT 15 1991

Mr. David Kilgour, M.P.
House of Commons
Ottawa, K1A 0A6

Dear Mr. Kilgour:

Thank you for your letter of August 21, 1991, concerning Mr. ███████████.

I have been informed that Treasury Board has now approved the proposed settlement and that the cheque is being prepared. The cheque as well as release documents will be forwarded to Mr. ████████ counsel in the very near future, if this has not already been done.

Yours sincerely,

A. Kim Campbell

Ottawa, Canada K1A 0H8

Appendix 2

Terry Mallenby went off his Canada Pension Plan disability pension first approved in 1979, thinking the RCMP harassment may have finished?

However, he was unable to cover-up for an apparent "sleeze ball", as cited in the current author's new book:

BOOK SUPPRESSED BY "HITLER" HARPER!
Whistleblower! And darn proud of it!

As cited, this 'little guy' who lost a job after blowing the whistle on the Whitbourne Centre to Premier Clyde Wells and Social Services Minister Kay Young, had warned these two "idiot" politicians of the dangers at the Whitbourne Centre![1]

However, they wouldn't listen [just like all the Whistelblowers cited in this book and elsewhere[2]] and got rid of their own whistleblower only to find out a year later that a tragedy did occur at the Whitbourne Centre!

With the Newfoundland there was a Whistleblower who wrote to Newfoundland Premier Clyde Wells and to Newfoundland Social Services Minister Kay Young telling them that the security at the maximum security youth centre, the Whitbourne Centre, was lax and should be improved.[3]

What did Newfoundland Premier Clyde Wells and Newfoundland Social Services Minister Kay Young do?

They didn't listen to the Whistleblower; instead they fabricated some cock-and-bull excuse and got rid of him, just like all the government ministers and managers cited in this book and elsewhere.[4]

And what did that "sleaze-ball" Social Services Minister Kay Young do; she even violated the violation of the Freedom of Information Act and the Privacy Act to make sure this whistleblowers was good-and-gone!

Can't have anyone blowing the whistle on political / government incompetence can we:

November 16, 1994
HOUSE OF ASSEMBLY PROCEEDINGS
Vol. XLII No. 62
http://www.assembly.nl.ca/business/hansard/ga42session2/94-11-16.htm

MR. FITZGERALD: Thank you, Mr. Speaker.

My question is to the Minister of Social Services. I want to ask the Minister of Social Services why she released information on the employment history of a Mr. xx, the former operations manager at the Newfoundland and Labrador Youth Centre, in clear violation of the Freedom of Information Act and in violation I believe of the Privacy Act?

MR. FITZGERALD: Mr. Speaker, not only did the minister violate the Freedom of Information and Privacy Act but she also gave false information, Mr. Speaker, about Mr. xx's employment history. The minister said that Mr. xx had been fired for reasons related to job performance. The official record of employment the department gave to Mr. xx and to Employment Canada says he was dismissed for breach of trust and loss of confidence. Now I ask the minister, did the minister know, Mr. Speaker, that she was giving false information in her press release? <u>Will she now admit Mr. xx was fired because he blew the whistle and disclosed the information as to what was actually happening out at the Newfoundland and Labrador Youth Centre</u>?

Now comes that "sleaze-ball" Newfoundland Premier Clyde Wells:

November 17, 1994
HOUSE OF ASSEMBLY PROCEEDINGS
Vol. XLII No. 63
http://www.assembly.nl.ca/business/hansard/ga42session2/94-11-17.htm

MR. W. MATTHEWS: Thank you very much, Mr. Speaker.

I have a question for the Premier, following up on the line of questioning by the member for Bonavista South yesterday dealing with the Minister of Social Services Kay Young. Now, on November 8, 1994 the Minister of Social Services Kay Young issued a public statement, a written press release, where she referred to the dismissal of one Mr. xx at the Newfoundland and Labrador Youth Center at Whitbourne. In that she talked about the reasons for dismissal, job performance and work history.

I want to ask the Premier, in light of the minister's public statement that is clearly a violation of the Freedom of Information Act and the Privacy Act, but particularly the Freedom Information Act, section 10 (1) (b): Does the Premier consider this conduct and behavior of the Minister of Social Services Kay Young to be acceptable?

MR. W. MATTHEWS: - and in that written, deliberate statement pertaining to the situation, she said: Mr. xx was dismissed for work related problems, job performance. Now the record of employment belonging to

Mr. xx states that he was dismissed for breach of trust and loss of confidence, so in essence, the minister in her statement, issued a false statement. The reason was inaccurate and incorrect, so I want to ask the Premier: does he feel that the conduct of the Minister of Social Services Kay Young, in issuing a false, public statement is behaviour and conduct acceptable for a minister of his Administration or, is he going to allow the standards and behaviour and conduct of the ministers to sink to an all-time low in this Province, where, individual privacy will no longer be protected?

What happened a year later, due to the lax security, one of the youth committed suicide and a stink was raised about Newfoundland Premier Clyde Wells and Newfoundland Social Services Minister Kay Young ignoring these Whistleblower warnings!

BOOK SUPPRESSED BY "HITLER" HARPER!
Terry Mallenby Successfully Sued the RCMP:
Newfoundland Kay Young reveals PTSD sufferers name to media

Footnotes

1. *The Newfoundland Department of Social Services is the worst department this author has ever read about*, AMICUS No. 16972196, National Library of Canada.

2. *Some Canadian Whistleblowers*
Topics: Whistleblowers
http://fairwhistleblower.ca/wbers/canadian_wbs.html

3. *The Newfoundland Department of Social Services is the worst department this author has ever read about*, AMICUS No. 16972196, National Library of Canada.

4. *Some Canadian Whistleblowers*
Topics: Whistleblowers
http://fairwhistleblower.ca/wbers/canadian_wbs.html

Newfoundland's Premier Kathy Dunderdale doesn't want to hear about the lies by Clyde Wells and by the Royal Canadian Mounted Police!!

Similarily, the following "great" provincial politicians of Newfoundland also did not want to hear about the lies by Clyde Wells, Kay Young and the Royal Canadian Mounted police – so these Newfoundland Politicians blocked the author's emails to them??

Incredibly apparently including the Premier of Newfoundland??

This is an automatically generated Delivery Status Notification.
Delivery to the following recipients failed.
kathydunderdale@gov.nl.ca

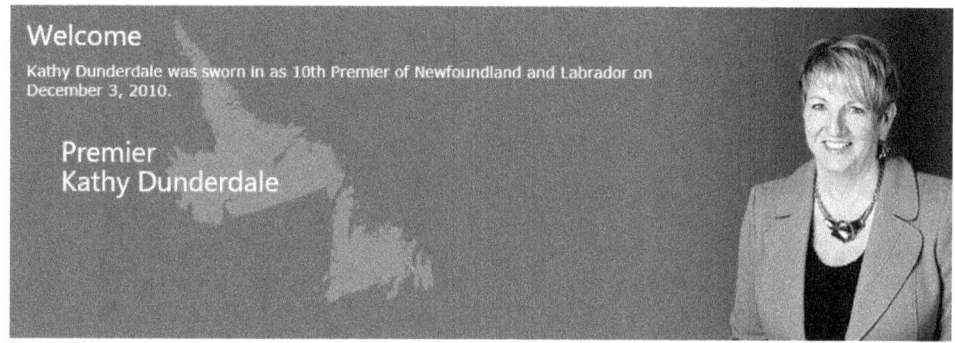

Honourable Kathy Dunderdale
Premier of Newfoundland and Labrador

Kathy Dunderdale was sworn in as the 10th Premier of Newfoundland and Labrador on December 3, 2010, and on October 11, 2011, became the first female ever elected premier of the province, and the second woman elected to a premiership in Canada.

Premier Dunderdale grew up in the town of Burin, Newfoundland and Labrador.

She attended Memorial University and worked throughout the province in the fields of community development, communications, fisheries and social work.

Appendix 3a

Terry Mallenby was diagnosed with a multitude of disorders as a consequence of RCMP and Federal Government illegal acts, harassment and other abuse.

Author's note: Anyone who has to identify a loved-one in the morgue can appreciate the horror, grief, anger one experiences?

September 24th, 1996

The Medical Advisor
Income Security Programs
333 River Rd
Ottawa, Ontario
K1A 9Z9

OCT 7 1996

Dear Sir or Madame:

Re:

I am writing a letter on behalf of   one of my patients who suffers from a grievous mental malady. He has been previously accepted for CPP disability.

His case is complicated. He is a very accomplished gentleman who has two advanced degrees including a Ph.D. and yet cannot work. He spends his time largely sequestered at home writing notes and letters and suffers extreme anxiety if he attempts to go outside.

He is very secretive about events that happened in the past but evidently he sustained a major personal loss in 1976 and ever since then has never recovered. He has paranoid ideas and symptoms of marked anxiety. I have been treating him as best I could as a family physician but felt his symptoms were aggravated and complicated enough that I referred him to a psychiatrist.

suffers from many symptoms of post-traumatic stress disorder and unresolved grief.....fear, guilt, horror, dreams of traumatic content, social avoidancy, decreased interest, impaired memory, irritability, anger, increased vigilance, sense of futility regarding the future, some paranoid ideations.

Appendix 3b

Author's note: Anyone who has to identify a loved-one in the morgue can appreciate the horror, grief, anger one experiences?

October 17, 1996

FRANCOISE LeBLANC, R.N., B.A.,
DISABILITY OPERATIONS DIVISION
333 RIVER ROAD
OTTAWA, CANADA   K1A 0L1

RE:

Dear Francoise,

Thank you for your letter of October 1, 1996

          gives a 20 year history of Post-Traumatic Stress Disorder following the homicide of a colleague in a prison uprising and also the murder   in 1976. I believe you are well aware of these events and that   was falsely accused of the latter crime. The effect on his family relationships and on him are also well documented.   has become very suspicious of others especially Government agencies and is somewhat paranoid. This paranoia has made it difficult for him to accept psychological help as a degree of trust is almost essential. He seems to have made numerous attempts to improve his occupational situation, but his difficulties dealing with others always overwhelm him.

When seen,   exhibited and described numerous signs and symptoms of Post-Traumatic Stress Disorder including marked agitation whenever the subject of the murder loomed. He described fear, guilt and horror, traumatic dreams, social avoidance, loss of interest, poor memory for details of the murder, irritability, anger, increased vigilance, a sense of futility re. the future, difficulties with emotional involvement, and arousal by recollections of the trauma including those precipitated by news stories of similar events. In interviews, he is often tearful ,distraught and agitated.

Diagnostically, he has   1)   Post-Traumatic Stress Disorder -Chronic Type
                                2)   Social Phobia -secondary to 1)

Appendix 3c

Terry Mallenby was diagnosed with a multitude of disorders as a consequence of RCMP and Federal Government illegal acts, harassment and other abuse.

April 1, 1998

To   Mr. Denis Duhamel
     Tower A, 11th floor
     Place Vanier

From: Dr. N. Kanjilal
       Medical Advisor

Subject:

As per your request, I reviewed the file of   to determine the basis for granting him the disability benefits.

You are well aware that we are guided by the CPP Legislation which states that a person must be suffering from a physical and/or mental disability which is both severe and prolonged to be eligible to receive disability benefits. Severe means that the person must be incapable of pursuing any substantially gainful occupation regularly. Prolonged means that the incapacity to work at any substantially gainful occupation will likely be long continued and of indefinite duration. To assess such disability we have to ascertain the limiting loss or absence of the capacity to meet the occupational demands according to the regulatory requirements described above.

seems to have satisfied the legislation and in our judgement he is incapable to carry out any occupational demands.

will be well advised to consult his treating physicians if he wishes to find out about any particular medical condition, who will be in a better position to explain his specific question.

Hope this answers some of your problems. Please do not hesitate to contact me should you need any other information.

Dr. N. Kanjilal
Tel: 952-3620

61

Chapter 9

Skunks in our village can't hide forever!

Someone contacted the author to say where John (Jack) Thomas Randle is living –in Hope, British Columbia, Canada!!

As mentioned, Terry Mallenby took on some slimy bastards and won!

RCMP Staff Sgt John Thomas Randle was the original RCMP LIAR who said the husband was an unwilling witness at the 1976 Squamish, British Columbia, Canada inquest!

As can be seen in text, Terry Mallenby has the original Coroner Inquest report sent to him by the Coroner's office clearly indicating he was not an unwilling witness!!

In fact, the Coroner apologized to Terry Mallenby for listening to the Police lies that he was an "unwilling witness"!

Staff Sgt John Thomas Randle was the RCMP "arse hole" who wrote a letter in 1979 saying the husband was a murderer!

And to prove that Staff Sgt John Thomas Randle was not only a LIAR but a big, fat "arse hole" – Terry Mallenby used Randle's big fat lies to successfully sue the Queen of England, the Canada Government and the Royal Canadian Mounted Police, including John Thomas (Jack) Randle!!

And Terry Mallenby received a $275,000 out of court settlement due to the lies of RCMP Jack Randle!!

Thanks "arse hole" RCMP Jack Randle – the money has come in handy!!

Terry Mallenby also used RCMP John Thomas Randle's lies to be approved for a PTSD [Post-Tramatic Stress Disorder] pension, which he has received since he was age 28!

The person that contacted the author didn't have a high regard for this former RCMP Officer John Thomas (Jack) Randle!!

The person said that apparently Jack Randle is 76 years old. He had Connections with Lethbridge, Alberta, Canada and maybe Creston, British Columbia, Canada.

Jack Randle also apparently ran a Meat & Deli shop in Richmond, British Columbia, Canada.

However, now Jack Randle makes his home in Hope, British Columbia, Canada where he was apparently in the motel business up until 5 years ago.

He is also listed as the President of Coquihalla Intercare Society:
1225 7th Ave RR 4, Hope, BC V0X 1L4
604-869-5046

The person that contacted the author thought that former RCMP Officer John Thomas (Jack) Randle was a miserable shite!!

Did RCMP John (Jack) Thomas Randle abandon son at birth – and after son tracked the "dead-beat" down – Randle has steadfastly refused to talk to the boy?

The fellow that phoned about Randle seemed to have found some information about the "dead-beat"?

← PERSONAL & CONFIDENTIAL

Sent to **brian.jean@parl.gc.ca** on **Dec 30, 2013, 5:39 AM**

Brian Jean, MP
102-9912 Franklin Avenue
Fort Mcmurray, Alberta T9H 2K4
Telephone: 780-743-2201
brian.jean@parl.gc.ca
brian.jean.c1@parl.gc.ca
brian.jean.c2@parl.gc.ca

Dear MP Brian Jean,

I received a phone call from a person who said you and he were "boyhood" friends [I'm not sure of the spelling of his name].

He believes all evidence points to former RCMP S/S John Thomas Randle [Jack Randle] as being his biological father, but apparently Jack Randle won't give this fellow the time-of-day.

Like all abandoned children this young fellow wanted to about Jack Randle's health history as do most abandoned children who track down their biological parents!

Did this guy Randle help the young fellow, no way not this "turd"!!

Go f--- yourself was Randle's reply and leave him alone!!!

Is this a photo of retired S/Sgt. Jack Randle

This apparent son of RCMP S/S John Thomas Randle said he had checked Randle out thoroughly and he said Randle ran a motel in Hope, British Columbia, Canada:

(a)   *Mr. Jack Randle*
        Re: OHPW Revitalization Project – Improved Street Lighting

Mr. Jack Randle of the Colonial 900 Motel stated that the Ministry of Highways advised them that the street lighting will only be going to Riverside Manor and/or the Coquihalla Motel.

Colonial 900 Motel
Contact Person : John Randle
Employees: 1 to 4
Sales: Less than $500,000
900 Old Hope Princeton Way,
 PO Box 849, Hope, BC, Canada V0X 1L0
Tel 1-604-869-5223
Fax 1-604-869-5228
E-mail 900motel@gmail.com

Reader's Comment about RCMP and guy's like this Randle, ironically by, Clayton Randle, Langley:

Clayton Randle, Langley

No! The RCMP is like a ship without a rudder. No accountability, no leadership, no direction from Parliament and a dysfunctional justice system has paralyzed the RCMP.

In an ideal world, an all-in-one municipal, provincial and national police force might work, but conditions are not ideal, and it isn't working. We have to review our national security needs and then develop a national strategy to provide the service.

With Stephen Harper being the biggest liability in this equation, that will not happen soon.

Here's another apparent skunk with the RCMP!

"RCMP Inspector Accused Of Groping Civilian Employees"
CBC | Posted: 06/18/2012

RCMP in Ottawa are investigating one of their own inspectors after two civilian employees raised complaints about inappropriate touching at a recent regimental event.

The women allege Insp. Brian Redmond groped them at a dinner held for around 100 employees at RCMP "A" Division in Ottawa on April 20.

The women have alleged Redmond, the division's intelligence officer, got drunk and patted or slapped their rear ends.

Redmond already has a reputation for dishonourable behaviour. CBC

News obtained two previous RCMP adjudication board reports outlining how in 2000 and 2001, when Redmond ran the Mounties' undercover training operations, he had sex with one of his female students and intimate relations with three other women.

When another candidate on the course reported the sexual relations to a supervisor, Redmond and the supervisor cooked up a scheme to ensure the man passed the course even though he had been found unsuitable for undercover duties.

The adjudication report also describes how, when the RCMP investigated those allegations, Redmond tried to intimidate one of the investigators and made false statements to two others.

What's the deal with these RCMP "Sexual Perverts" – get the girl pregnant and   then abandon her??

Is that what happened to RCMP S/S John Thomas Randle, he got some girl pregnant and then abandoned his son at birth???

After all, what kind of "skunk" doesn't talk to his own son – once the son has tracked him down??

Chapter 2 – Part 3

A village where senators obey the law!

None of our village senators would do what this senator did, would they?

Senator Larry Campbell, former Chief Coroner, former RCMP Officer says he doesn't give a shite about 1976 Squamish Coroner Inquest Judgement – the Royal Canadian Mounted Police will harass Terry Mallenby, his wife and children forever!!

The Royal Canadian Mounted Police doesn't like the fact that Terry Mallenby successfully sued them!

So what did they do, they uploaded their 1976 lies when Terry Mallenby was age 28 and again in 2012 when Terry Mallenby was age 65??

Let's first define a Coroner's Inquest in British Columbia Canada.

Coroner's Inquest

An inquest is held and a Verdict at Inquest is written. Inquests are formal court proceedings, with a five-person jury, held to publicly review the circumstances of a death. The jury hears evidence from witnesses under subpoena in order to determine the facts of the death.

The Coroner is responsible for ascertaining the facts surrounding a death and must determine:

- The identity of the deceased.
- How, when, where and by what means the deceased died.

The death is then classified as natural, accidental, suicide, homicide or undetermined.

So what have the RCMP done, they have uploaded their 1976 lies that Terry Mallenby was an unwilling witness:

Husband reluctant witness .at Mallenby inquest - digitalcollections.ca
www.digitalcollections.ca/.../r/.../19760401_Squamish_Times.pdf

However, as can be seen below, the author has the original Coroner Inquest report sent to him by the Coroner's office of British Columbia Canada!!

Province of
British Columbia

Solicitor General
B.C. CORONERS SERVICE

4595 Canada Way
Burnaby
British Columbia
V5G 4L9
Phone (604) 660-7700

March 1, 1989

Mr. Terry Mallenby
C.P. 2181
Dorval, P.Q.
H9S 3K9

Dear Mr. Mallenby:

SUBJECT: Coroner's Inquest

As per your written request please find attached
a certified true copy of the transcript from the Inquest
into the unfortunate death of Ruth Mallenby. I trust this
transcript will provide you with the information that you
require.

Yours truly,

Debi Rupert
Secretary

/dr
Attachment

P. 300

68

Author's Note: The letters and numbers [P3ai] at the bottom of the above noted letter refers to the evidence the Terry Mallenby submitted to the Federal Court of Canada when he SUCCESSFULLY SUED the Royal Canadian Mounted Police!!

The RCMP didn't like this and has harassed the author, his wife and children since that time!!!

And they did that when they knew the author's lawyer was out of town in 1976??

DEFENCE

First of all in respect to the arrangements and the arrest of this man, he was not represented by counsel on any of the submissions and I would have respectfully would have desired an opportunity to have made that representation for him in respect to that warrant, that was issued

in respect to this matter. Secondly, I was completely unaware of the arrest.' I was at a location where a phone was not available readily, and I was not aware of the fact that this matter of the arrest had come on. It was not a question of arranging at my convenience, it was a matter of him appearing in my absence, and that knowledge that I was going to be absent for awhile was information that the Crown had.

DEFENCE

Mr. Coroner, there is one point I feel
I must raise before the jury are
excused. I wish to stress that I have
reviewed the transcript of the proceedings
of the last occasion we were here,
and I was disturbed in the extreme to
read of the comments made on the voluntari-
ness of my client and I feel that no
prejudicial leanings should be taken
from that. My client was not notified
or asked to appear.

Again, the author has to put the facts straight!!!

The verdict in this 1976 Coroner's Inquest – by persons or persons unknown:

.ERDICT   149

REMARKS   148
Inquest.)

CORONER   Has the jury reached a verdict?

We find that this death was unnatural and that it was homicide. We find that some person or persons unknown are to blame. We recommend that investigation be continued.

CORONER   Do you all so find?

JURORS   We do.

CORONER   Thank you gentlemen and ladies for your attendance her to-night.

L. C. KINDREE,   M.D.,
Coroner

I hereby certify the foregoing to
be a true and accurate transcript
of the proceedings herein to the
best of my skill and ability.

Evelyn A. McCartney,
Official Court Reporter.

So what have the RCMP done, they have put some more bull-shit about the Terry Mallenby – this time that he was an unwilling witness which is what the RCMP [through the Crown] told the Coroner in 1976!!!

DEFENCE

First of all in respect to the arrangements and the arrest of this man, he was not represented by counsel on any of the submissions and I would have respectfully would have desired an opportunity to have made that representation for him in respect to that warrant, that was issued

in respect to this matter. Secondly, I was completely unaware of the arrest.' I was at a location where a phone was not available readily, and I was not aware of the fact that this matter of the arrest had come on. It was not a question of arranging at my convenience, it was a matter of him appearing in my absence, and that knowledge that I was going to be absent for awhile was information that the Crown had.

DEFENCE

Mr. Coroner, there is one point I feel
I must raise before the jury are
excused. I wish to stress that I have
reviewed the transcript of the proceedings
of the last occasion we were here,
and I was disturbed in the extreme to
read of the comments made on the voluntari-
ness of my client and I feel that no
prejudicial leanings should be taken
from that. My client was not notified
or asked to appear.

Chapter 11

Why did our village senator say he doesn't care about the missing and murdered?

Well, here he is:

Larry W. Campbell - Liberal Party of Canada

Province: British Columbia
Senatorial Designation: British Columbia
Appointed on the advice of: Martin (Lib.)
Telephone: 613-995-4050 or 1-800-267-7362
Fax: 613-995-4056
Email: larry.campbell@sen.parl.gc.ca

References courtesy of the Fair Use Act, for research purposes, to clarify the author's point of view.

Biography

One of Vancouver's best-known and most admired citizens, Larry W. Campbell has served as mayor since 2002 after a distinguished and high profile career primarily in law enforcement and death investigation.

Author's Note: This Larry Campbell has a long career of law enforcement and death investigation, yet with respect to the missing and murdered in Squamish, British Columbia he says -

Yawn

Squamish again

Larry Campbell

Here's the missing and murdered in Squamish, British Columbia, Canada that Senator Larry Campbell, former RCMP officer, doesn't give "two hoots" about:

SQUAMISH # 1

Oct. 29, '85: Rachel Turley, 20
Turley's body was found in a wooded area near Squamish. She had been sexually assaulted, beaten and strangled. Police say she was known to them as a Granville Mall "street person" who once worked as a prostitute.

A 2001 Vancouver Sun article listing the missing
http://www.highwayoftears.ca/missingbclist.htm

SQUAMISH # 2

Topic: 1970's Squamish, BC - possible connection between 3 murders?
Re: 1970's Squamish, BC - possible connection between 3 murders?
« Reply #20 on: August 02, 2011, 04:19:55 PM »

I'm sorry about your friend. Sadly there were so many serial killers in this area during that era, it hard to know for sure.

Unsolved Murders | Missing People Canada
http://www.unsolvedcanada.ca/index.php?topic=3091.15

SQUAMISH # 3

Re: Jodi Henrickson~17~missing~Bowen Island/Squamish~June 20,2009
« Reply #61 on: May 23, 2012, 11:55:54 AM »
Body found on Bowen Island
By Jane Seyd, North Shore News May 23, 2012 6:34 AM

POLICE investigating the discovery of a body in a bushy area of Bowen Island say the remains are likely not those of missing Squamish teen Jodi Henrickson.

"We don't feel it's connected to that case," said Sgt. Jennifer Pound, spokeswoman for the RCMP's Integrated Homicide Investigation Team. Pound said investigators ruled out that the body was Henrickson early on, although she declined to say how police did that.

Bowen Island RCMP were called out Friday at around 2 p.m. by a local resident who had discovered the body on his land, a wooded property in the 1,000 block of Harding Road.

An autopsy is to be performed Tuesday to try to identify the victim and the likely cause of death. Suicide remains a possibility, as does the chance that the body was dumped there.

"There are no obvious signs of injury," said Pound.

So far investigators have not confirmed whether the body - which was badly decomposed - is male or female. "We believe the body was there for quite some time," said Pound.

Lloyd Harding, who lives on Harding Road, said he was walking down to his mailbox with his son's dog at the end of last week when the Jack Russell terrier tried to drag him into the bush.

Harding said he noticed a bad smell in the area. "I thought someone had hit a deer he said."

Harding said he's walked right by the area where the body was found before but didn't see anything or notice any smell in the area before last week's spell of hot weather.

Police are currently checking missing persons reports to see if they can help identify the remains.

Henrickson, then 17, disappeared three years ago on June 20, 2009 after leaving a house party on Bowen Island with her ex-boyfriend Gavin Arnott. Neither Henrickson nor any signs of her have shown up since then, despite several searches by both police and volunteers.

Police have repeatedly said they think Henrickson met with foul play and never left the island.

Harding said the quiet community is "shocked and very concerned" by Friday's discovery.

jseyd@nsnews.com

http://www.nsnews.com/news/Body+found+Bowen+Island/6663655/story.html

Unsolved Murders | Missing People Canada
http://www.unsolvedcanada.ca/index.php?topic=2890.60

SQUAMISH # 4

Christopher Leo Turgeon | 3 | Missing Squamish BC | December 18, 1999
« on: July 17, 2011, 10:39:27 PM »
Case Number: 0000110

Missing Since: 18 December 1999
Missing From: Squamish, British Columbia, CANADA
Details: Christopher was abducted by his non-custodial mother, Lilia VAZQUEZ.
Missing Child:

Christopher Leo TURGEON
Date of Birth: 14 March 1996
Sex: Male
Hair: Brown
Eye: Brown
Height: 91 cm (36 feet, inches)
Weight: 19 kg (42 lb)
Additional Information: He has a mole on his lower lip on the right side. He speaks English and Spanish. Christopher's photo is age-progressed to 7 years old.

May be in the company of:

Lilia Martinez VAZQUEZ
Date of Birth: 23 March 1974
Sex: Female
Hair: Brown
Eye: Brown
Height: 173 cm (68 feet, inches)
Weight: 50 kg (110 lb)
Additional Information: The abductor was born in Mexico. She speaks Spanish and English.
Alias(es): Lilia MARTINEZ, Lilia MARTINEZ VAZQUEZ, Lilia VASQUEZ

Relationship: Mother
http://www.ourmissingchildren.gc.ca/cgi-bin/case.pl?id=181&lang=eng

Unsolved Murders | Missing People Canada
http://www.unsolvedcanada.ca/index.php?topic=5195.0

SQUAMISH # 5

Re: 1950 - 1969 Unsolved Murders and Missing - Canada

« Reply #45 on: April 11, 2010, 06:18:24 PM »

Furry Creek, BC Okay, I am going to post some more of my findings, unfortunately, not much to find. I will post the info over a few posts. This first lot is not in the date sequence as originally listed. I may have found a common thread in these ones. Although they are listed as Squamish/Vancouver cases, when I looked at the death registration information on Ancestry.ca I found all of their locations of death were within 18km of a place called Furry Creek, BC. I have included one that was listed as Squamish as it seems to be in the same area. I am not sure if these young ladies actually died/were found near Furry Creek or if they were perhaps, from there, and therefore, their deaths were listed for that location. I have to break this one into two posts as the computer is fussing

1. 12 April 73 Helen Hopcroft, age 17, Vancouver
    Her death was registered as 13 May 73, Furry Creek, BC
    There was an obituary for her in the Winnipeg Free Press 7 June 73

2. 17 Feb 75 Gayle Rogers, Vancouver, BC
    If it is the same young lady, found "Gail Sandra Rogers" Date of registered death, 7 Mar 75, she was born in 1949 so she was 26,
    her death is registered as "Squamish, BC"

Unsolved Murders | Missing People Canada
http://www.unsolvedcanada.ca/index.php?topic=416.45

SQUAMISH # 6

Fraser Member
Posts: 120
« Reply #46 on: April 11, 2010, 06:27:30 PM »

Furry Creek cont'd

3. 25 Jan 75 Margie Melinda Blackwell, 21
   Death registration: 25 Jan 75, place of death, Furry Creek, BC

4. 26 Feb 76 Ruth Gwendolyn Mallenby, 26, Squamish
    Death Registration: "Ruth Gwendelyne Mallenby", 7 Mar 76 Lion's Bay, (18 km from Furry Creek, BC)

For everyone's consideration. If I find anymore with this link I will add them to this post.

Unsolved Murders | Missing People Canada
http://www.unsolvedcanada.ca/index.php?topic=416.45

SQUAMISH # 7

Sunday afternoon a group of hikers found a dead body near a hiking trail on the side of Mamquam Road in Squamish. "It appears the man was met with foul play," said spokeswoman Sgt. Jennifer Pound. "It does appear to be a homicide." Pound also refused to comment on media reports that the man's body was found beaten and duct-taped.

Kim Bolan has reported the identity of the body is that of William Woo from Surrey who was an associate of the East Vancouver hells angels but more recently went over to the other side. Now he's in a body bag. I wonder who the prime suspects are? If the East Vancouver chapter of the Hells angels contract a murder, that makes them a criminal organization guilty of murder. I don't know about the Duhre Daiquiris but Lotus, now there is some old school credibility right there. They are more than capable of professional payback.

Beaten and duck taped. Yeah that would imply foul play. It reminds me of two other cases in Squamish. One was a guy named Alex Larsen who was run over by a truck because he was lying in the middle of the road. It's so strange and tragic. Yes it's possible he got drunk or high and passed out. Yet we've never heard a word either way. We don't know if he was beaten and dumped there or if he was walking on the side of the road and a car hit him which was why he was lying in the middle of the road before the bus ran him over. The case comes to mind and I wish there was more pieces to that puzzle. They say he had made a decision to turn his life around. Just like Britney Irving. Tragic indeed.

Of course there's that other bizarre case in Squamish, the murder of Javan Luke Dowling. Three drug dealers were driving in a car in Vancouver. One of the drug dealers, shot one of the other drug dealers in the head and the third drug dealer watched the shooter cut off Dowling's head and dismembered his body. The two surviving drug dealers buried the body in two separate locations in Squamish. Mihaly Illes was alleged to be the shooter while Derrick Madinski helped him bury the body. Derrick Madinski went with Joe Brallic to LA where Joe was ripped off and murdered.

Meanwhile in that same original article about a new dead body being found in Squamish it later stated there was another shooting in Surrey near the corner of 111A Avenue and 146th Street at about 2: 40 a.m. on Sunday. It didn't even make it's own head line. Kinda sad. The point is violent crime is continuing and as the papers also report the court system is currently in crisis. That was before Harper's disproportionate crime bill sent the fragile system into chaos.

Gangsters Out Blog
http://gangstersout.blogspot.ca/2011/10/body-dumped-in-squamish.html

Chapter 2 – Part 5

Our village senator wasn't a "pot-head" was he?

As further stated about the guy:

Larry W. Campbell moved to Vancouver in 1969, working for the RCMP and later becoming a member of the force's Drug Squad. In 1981, he began work for the Government of British Columbia's Ministry of Attorney General!

Well, on Thursday, March 1, 2012 Senator Larry W. Campbell rose in the Senate and challenged two other Senators:

Hon. Larry W. Campbell: Honourable senators, I rise today to speak on Bill C-10, the safe streets and communities act. Before I start, I will have to invite Senator Nolin and Senator Runciman to the province of British Columbia so that I can show them that, on Galiano Island at least, we are safe and that the crime rate has not risen substantially over the past few years.

Sounds impressive, doesn't it??

Well, until you scratch the surface!!

First of all, Galiano Island had a population growth of only from 909 to 1071 from 1991 to 2001?

WHAT??

Whereas Senator Nolin's "riding" of De Salaberry, Québec, Canada had as of the 2011 Census a population of 40,077.

And, Senator Runciman "riding" of Leeds – Grenville, Ontario, Canada as of 2001 had a population of 96,606!!

Talk about not playing fair Senator Larry W. Campbell!!

Compare your "piddly little" Galiano Island, with a population of around 1,000 to other Senators with 40,077 and 96,606 populations restively??

Is this Senator Larry W. Campbell "out to lunch"???

In any event, let's examine Senator Larry W. Campbell assertions that his Galiano Island is free of crime!!

Well, the first thing one finds about Galiano Island is an article about the Marijuana grow ops on Galiano Island, British Columbia, Canada?

References courtesy of the Fair Use Act, for research purposes, to clarify the author's point of view

Light Action
May 6, 2011 - Uploaded by GIFTS Films
This video mini-doc explores Marijuana grow ops on Galiano Island, BC.
www.youtube.com/watch?v=ilPWt-E2jD4

WHAT??

Didn't it say:

Larry W. Campbell moved to Vancouver in 1969, working for the RCMP and later becoming a member of the force's Drug Squad. In 1981, he began work for the Government of British Columbia's Ministry of Attorney General!

And, in spite of this, the first thing one reads about Galiano Island is an article about the Marijuana grow ops on Galiano Island, British Columbia, Canada?

What was Senator Larry W. Campbell doing when he was with the Royal Canadian Mounted Police drug squad??

Sleeping on the job??

Or, just ignoring the Marijuana grow ops on Galiano Island, British Columbia, Canada?

After all, there are tons of photos of the "pot plants" on Galiano Island, British Columbia, Canada on the Internet:

More "pot plants" on Galiano Island, British Columbia, Canada on the Internet?

What was Senator Larry W. Campbell doing when he was with the Royal Canadian Mounted Police drug squad??

Sleeping on the job??

More "pot plants" on Galiano Island, British Columbia, Canada on the Internet?

What was Senator Larry W. Campbell doing when he was with the Royal Canadian Mounted Police drug squad??

Sleeping on the job??

More Marijuana "grow ops" on Galiano Island, British Columbia, Canada?

What was Senator Larry W. Campbell doing when he was with the Royal Canadian Mounted Police drug squad??

Sleeping on the job??

And this guy was the Attorney General of British Columbia, Canada entrusted with the task of prosecuting crime:

Larry W. Campbell moved to Vancouver in 1969, working for the RCMP and later becoming a member of the force's Drug Squad. In 1981, he began work for the Government of British Columbia's Ministry of Attorney General!

Yet, as one person said:

Will Emdomain
3 Sep 2013
https://plus.google.com/communities/107745936248739775285#communit
ies/107745936248739775285

And I own a house on Galiano Island, the RCMP officers that come onto the island know who grows.

They could just drive onto the property!!

And in terms of any of these Marijuana grow ops on Galiano Island, British Columbia, Canada being "busted", the same person writes:

I haven't heard of one in almost 15 years in the South Gulf Islands (BC).

WHAT??

Larry W. Campbell was the Attorney General of British Columbia, Canada entrusted with the task of prosecuting crime and there hasn't been a "bust" of Marijuana grow-ops on his Galiano Island!!

This guy wasn't sleeping on the job – as being blind, dumb, and stupid!!

Or, was he in cahoots with these Marijuana grow-ops, people used to say that the RCMP would supply protection for trucks with tarps over them coming out of the woods??

Others in British Columbia Canada have also said the RCMP are involved in the trafficking of Marijuana?

Rumours, or fact – especially when one resident says:

I haven't heard of one in almost 15 years in the South Gulf Islands (BC).

Someone is obviously protecting the Marijuana grow ops!!!

Chapter 13

Our village chief of police is law abiding!

RCMP Commissioner Robert Paulson upload 40 year old lies as RCMP payback because Terry Mallenby successfully sued them!!!

Anything is possible with this guy – He has no scruples!

In 1976 the Royal Canadian Mounted Police [RCMP] lied to the British Columbia Coroner in Squamish saying that Terry Mallenby was an unwilling witness [so they could arrest him]!!!

The Coroner apologized to Terry Mallenby for listening to the RCMP that he was an "unwilling witness"!

Because of the RCMP lies, Terry Mallenby missed his wife's funeral!

Terry Mallenby will hate the RCMP until the day he dies!

And Terry Mallenby will have books written about the RCMP scum to show the kind of "shit" they pull on the "little people"

And this book is just one in a series that tells the bitter truth about the RCMP!

Terry Mallenby eventually found a decent Canadian lawyer [they are hard to come by] who sued the RCMO, the Queen and the Canadian government [on a contingency basis] with Terry Mallenby winning a $275,000 out of court settlement.

The RCMP have been harassing Terry Mallenby, his wife and children ever since!!!

Terry Mallenby has been writing about the stupid bastards ever since:

> BOOK SUPPRESSED BY "HITLER" HARPER!
> *Canada's Police Force: Lies, fabrication, perjury ... and much worse?*
> *"Before his death he was able to tell a nurse at the hospital that an RCMP officer jumped up and down on him"*

Terry Mallenby successfully sued RCMP!

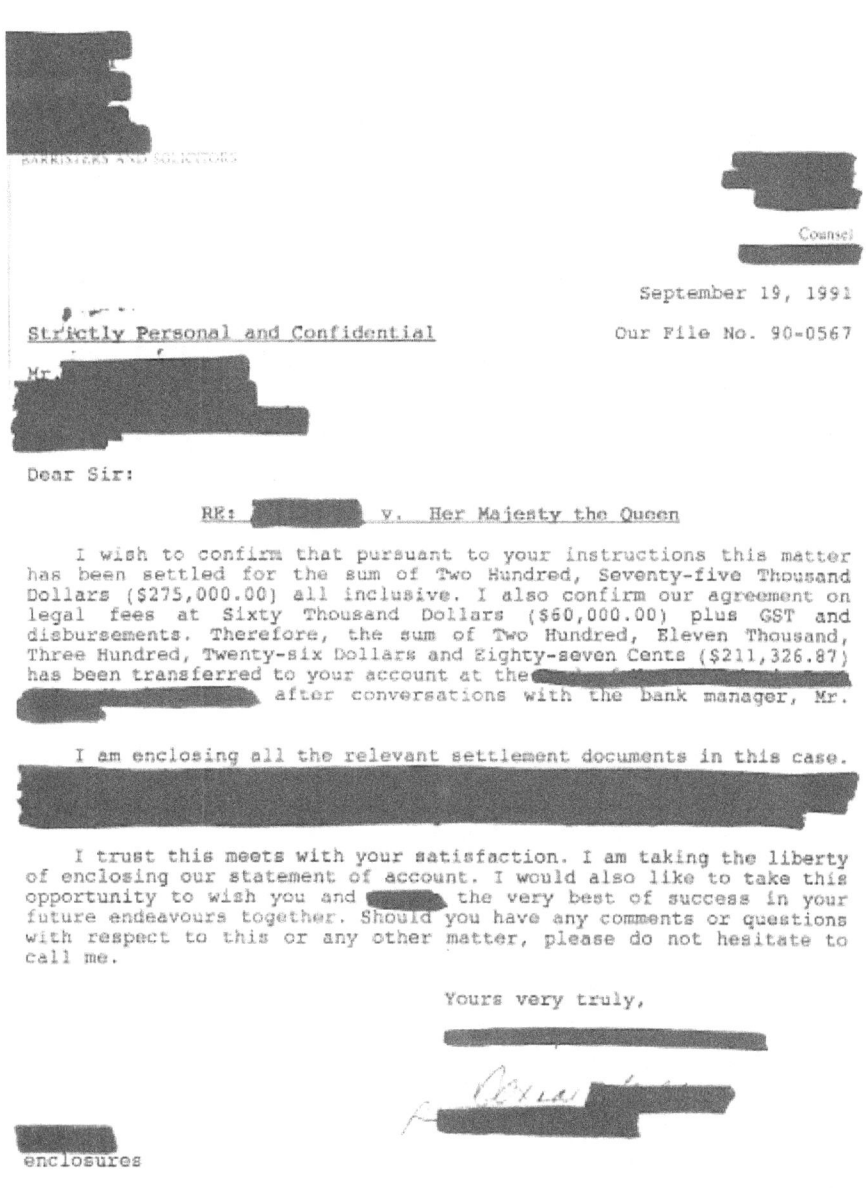

BARRISTERS AND SOLICITORS

Counsel

September 19, 1991

<u>Strictly Personal and Confidential</u>

Our File No. 90-0567

Mr.

Dear Sir:

RE: v. Her Majesty the Queen

    I wish to confirm that pursuant to your instructions this matter has been settled for the sum of Two Hundred, Seventy-five Thousand Dollars ($275,000.00) all inclusive. I also confirm our agreement on legal fees at Sixty Thousand Dollars ($60,000.00) plus GST and disbursements. Therefore, the sum of Two Hundred, Eleven Thousand, Three Hundred, Twenty-six Dollars and Eighty-seven Cents ($211,326.87) has been transferred to your account at the ███████████████████ after conversations with the bank manager, Mr.

    I am enclosing all the relevant settlement documents in this case.

    I trust this meets with your satisfaction. I am taking the liberty of enclosing our statement of account. I would also like to take this opportunity to wish you and ████████ the very best of success in your future endeavours together. Should you have any comments or questions with respect to this or any other matter, please do not hesitate to call me.

Yours very truly,

enclosures

Ottawa Ontario ████ Fax (613) ████ Telephone: (613) ████

Terry Mallenby successfully sued RCMP!

No: T-1131 93

IN THE FEDERAL COURT OF CANADA
TRIAL DIVISION

BETWEEN:

████████████,

and

Plaintiffs

AND:

HER MAJESTY THE QUEEN, ROYAL CANADIAN
MOUNTED POLICE and J.I. RANDLE.

Defendants

DECLARATION OF SETTLEMENT

The parties, by their counsel, hereby declare that the
present case has now been settled, each party paying its own costs.

SIGNED in Montreal, this ____
day of September 1991 ____

Terry Mallenby successfully sued RCMP!

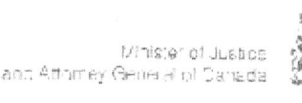

Minister of Justice
and Attorney General of Canada

Ministre de la Justice
et Procureur général du Canada

A. Kim Campbell, P.C., Q.C., M.P/o p., c.r., députée

OCT 15 1991

Mr. David Kilgour, M.P.
House of Commons
Ottawa, K1A 0A6

Dear Mr. Kilgour:

Thank you for your letter of August 21, 1991, concerning
Mr. ███████████.

I have been informed that Treasury Board has now approved
the proposed settlement and that the cheque is being prepared.
The cheque as well as release documents will be forwarded to
Mr. ███████ counsel in the very near future, if this has not
already been done.

Yours sincerely,

A. Kim Campbell

Ottawa, Canada K1A 0H8

Chapter 14

Our village leader would never do this!

Canadian Prime Minister "Hitler" Harper uploads 40 year old RCMP lies as RCMP payback because Terry Mallenby successfully sued the Federal Government of Canada??

Anything is possible with this guy!

Terry Mallenby successfully sued the Canadian Government!!

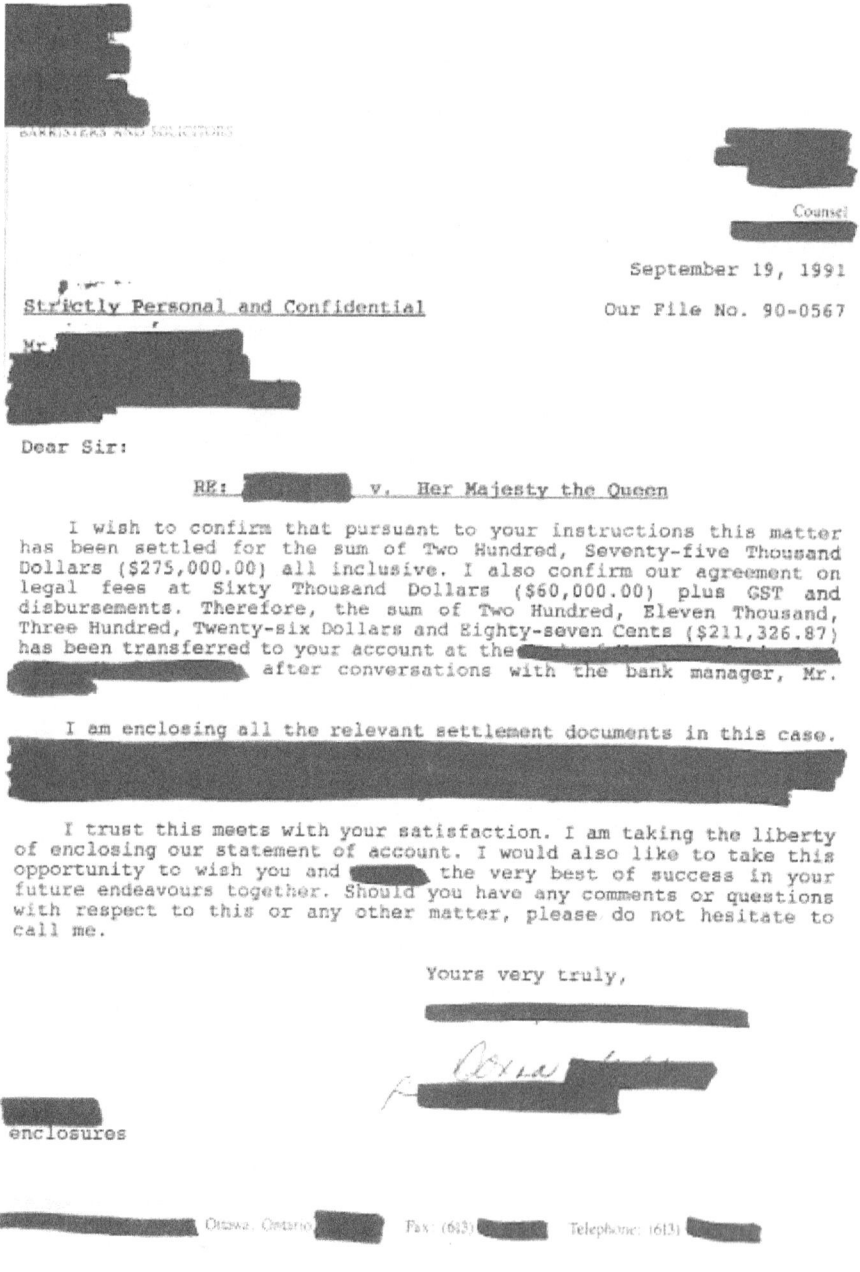

BARRISTERS AND SOLICITORS

Counsel

September 19, 1991

Strictly Personal and Confidential

Our File No. 90-0567

Mr.

Dear Sir:

RE: _____ v. Her Majesty the Queen

I wish to confirm that pursuant to your instructions this matter has been settled for the sum of Two Hundred, Seventy-five Thousand Dollars ($275,000.00) all inclusive. I also confirm our agreement on legal fees at Sixty Thousand Dollars ($60,000.00) plus GST and disbursements. Therefore, the sum of Two Hundred, Eleven Thousand, Three Hundred, Twenty-six Dollars and Eighty-seven Cents ($211,326.87) has been transferred to your account at the _____ after conversations with the bank manager, Mr.

I am enclosing all the relevant settlement documents in this case.

I trust this meets with your satisfaction. I am taking the liberty of enclosing our statement of account. I would also like to take this opportunity to wish you and _____ the very best of success in your future endeavours together. Should you have any comments or questions with respect to this or any other matter, please do not hesitate to call me.

Yours very truly,

enclosures

Ottawa, Ontario   Fax (613)   Telephone: (613)

Terry Mallenby successfully sued the Canadian Government!!

No: T-1131 93

IN THE FEDERAL COURT OF CANADA
TRIAL DIVISION

BETWEEN:

██████████ ,

and

Plaintiffs

AND:

HER MAJESTY THE QUEEN, ROYAL CANADIAN
MOUNTED POLICE and J.I. RANDLE.

Defendants

DECLARATION OF SETTLEMENT

The parties, by their counsel, hereby declare that the present case has now been settled, each party paying its own costs.

SIGNED in Montreal, this _____
day of September 1991 _____

Terry Mallenby successfully sued the Canadian Government!!

Minister of Justice
and Attorney General of Canada

Ministre de la Justice
et Procureur général du Canada

A. Kim Campbell, P.C., Q.C., M.P./c.p., c.r., députée

OCT 15 1991

Mr. David Kilgour, M.P.
House of Commons
Ottawa, K1A 0A6

Dear Mr. Kilgour:

Thank you for your letter of August 21, 1991, concerning
Mr. ███████████.

I have been informed that Treasury Board has now approved
the proposed settlement and that the cheque is being prepared.
The cheque as well as release documents will be forwarded to
Mr. ███████ counsel in the very near future, if this has not
already been done.

Yours sincerely,

A. Kim Campbell

RECEIVED · REÇU

OCT 18 1991

HOUSE OF COMMONS
Chambre des Communes

Ottawa, Canada K1A 0H8

94

Chapter 15

Our village leader loves Sanfu Chen and Darby Love!

As RCMP payback, Canadian Prime Minister "Hitler" Harper sent two fellow University of Alberta graduates all the way to Squamish, British Columbia, Canada [a distance of 1,223 km / 1,000 miles] to upload the same 40 year old RCMP lies about Terry Mallenby!!!

Why would Darby Love and Sanfu Chen both University of Alberta graduates travel all the way to Squamish British Columbia, Canada?

A distance of 1,223 km / 1,000 miles?

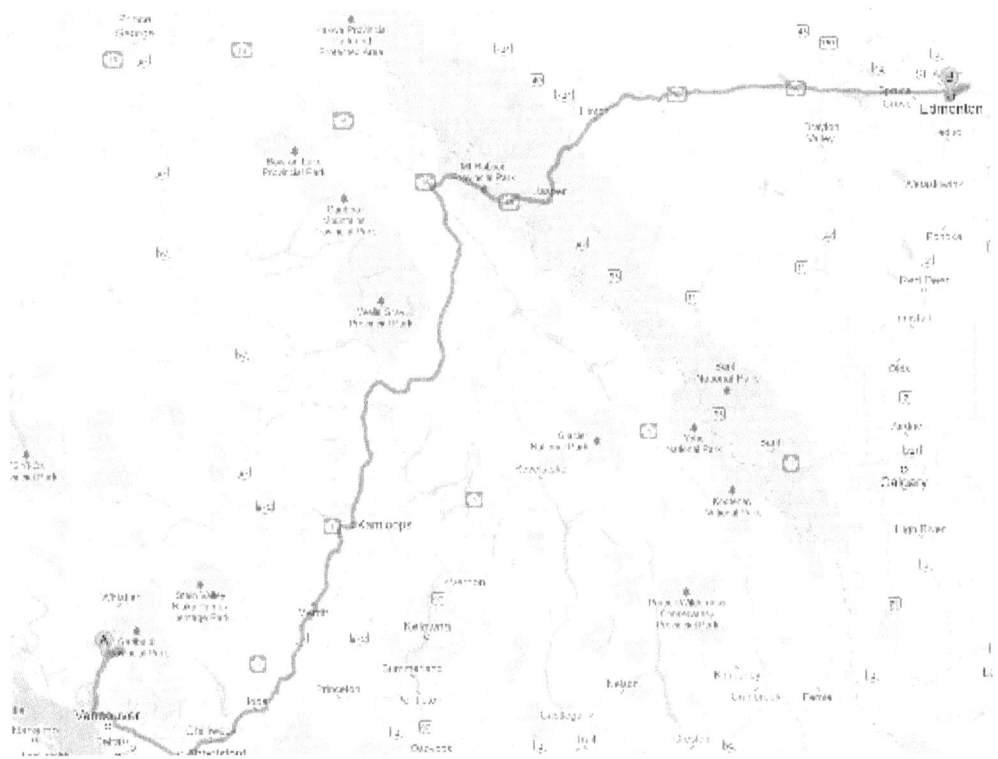

Why would a University of Alberta graduate travel all the way to Squamish British Columbia, Canada to upload one article from a non-existent newspaper to the internet?

"The company that owned the paper doesn't exist anymore so while the library has verbal permission to use the archives of the Squamish Times there is no formal document making it clear so an application is in front of the copyright board seeking formal acknowledgement that the library can publish the newspaper archive online, says Sanfu Chen."

Why because RCMP Commissioner Bob Paulson and Canadian Prime Minister Stephen Harper told them to upload the same 40 year old RCMP lies to keep Terry Mallenby, his wife and children unemployed!

Squamish Public Librarian Sanfu Chen uploaded 40 year old RCMP lies because RCMP Commissioner Bob Paulson and Canadian Prime Minister Stephen Harper told them to upload the same 40 year old RCMP lies to keep Terry Mallenby, his wife and children unemployed!!

Graduate student Sanfu Chen shifts through the Squamish Library's archives
Photo by Rebecca Aldous/The Chief

Squamish Public Librarian Sanfu Chen uploaded 40 year old RCMP lies because RCMP Commissioner Bob Paulson and Canadian Prime Minister Stephen Harper told them to upload the same 40 year old RCMP lies to keep Terry Mallenby, his wife and children unemployed!!

Historical Squamish photos and documents go online
Project awaiting word on next round of funding to carry on
by John French

Squamish Public Librarian Darby Love also uploaded 40 year old RCMP lies because RCMP Commissioner Bob Paulson and Canadian Prime Minister Stephen Harper told them to upload the same 40 year old RCMP lies to keep Terry Mallenby, his wife and children unemployed!!

Darby Love
Public Services Librarian at Squamish Public Library
Vancouver, Canada Area · Libraries

Darby Love, Reference Librarian
Squamish Public Library
37907 2nd Avenue, PO Box 1039
Squamish, BC V8B 0A7
dlove@squamish.ca
604-892-3110, ext. 5307

I live in a lovely village!

With trees, mountains, lakes and rivers …

A wondrous paradise …

Where everyone is treated equally …

Where no one is harassed …

Where the law applies to everyone …

Except this guy … because I published 40 year old lies about him to help our village leader and our village chief of police out!

Davide Burke

SOME ARTICLES PRIOR TO THE BRITISH COLUMBIA RCMP 1976 & 1979 LIES AND TERRY MALLENBY'S SUCCESSFUL SUIT AGAINST THE BRITISH COLUMBIA RCMP!!

Some articles by Terry Mallenby
former federal peace officer
old age pensioner & PTSD disability pensioner due to RCMP lies
former Classification Officer BC Maximum Security Penitentiary
former Classification Officer BC Medium Security Mountain Prison
former Probation Officer NFLD Social Services Department*
former Facility Operations Manager Whitbourne Youth Secure Custody

Cognitive development: the functional aspect of symbolization and language,
by Terry W Mallenby
OCLC Number: 1206866
Publisher: Winnipeg, S. Evans, ©1973.

A bibliography of research on spatial and social behaviour
by Terry W Mallenby
 OCLC Number: 1188853
Publisher: Winnipeg : Thomas Todd Press, 1973.

A bibliography of research on spatial behaviour.
by Terry W Mallenby; Ruth G Roberts
OCLC Number: 123780236
Publisher: Winnipeg : Thomas Todd Press, ©1973.

A note on perceived self-acceptance of institutionalized mentally retarded (IMR) children.
by TW Mallenby
ISSN: 0022-1325
OCLC Number: 105523657
Article
Language: English
Publication: The Journal of genetic psychology, 1973 Sep; 123(1st Half): 171-2
Database: From MEDLINE®/PubMed®, a database of the U.S. National Library of Medicine.

Personal space : direct measurement techniques with hard-of-hearing children
by Terry W Mallenby
OCLC Number: 8686052
From: Environment and behavior ; v. 6, no. 1 (March 1974).
Publisher: [Beverly Hills, CA] : Sage Publications, 1974.

Effect of discussion on reduction of magnitude of Poggendorff illusion.
by TW Mallenby
ISSN: 0031-5125
OCLC Number: 107527338
Publication: Perceptual and motor skills, 1974 Oct; 39(2): 787-91
Database: From MEDLINE®/PubMed®, a database of the U.S. National Library of Medicine.

Personal space: projective and direct measures with institutionalized mentally retarded children.
by TW Mallenby
ISSN: 0022-3891
OCLC Number: 105929976
Publication: Journal of personality assessment, 1974 Feb; 38(1): 28-31
Database: From MEDLINE®/PubMed®, a database of the U.S. National Library of Medicine.

Personal Space: Projective and Direct Measures with Institutionalized Mentally Retarded Children
by Terry Mallenby
ISSN: 0022-3891
OCLC Number: 4631503689
Publication: Journal of Personality Assessment, v38 n1 (19740201): 28-31
Database: ERIC The ERIC database is an initiative of the U.S. Department of Education.

Personal Space: Direct Measurement Techniques with Hard-of-Hearing Children
by Terry W Mallenby
OCLC Number: 424960945
Accession No: EJ098610
Publication: Environment and Behavior, 6, 1, 117-122, Mar 74
Database: ERIC The ERIC database is an initiative of the U.S. Department of Education.

MALLENBY, TERRY W., Personal Space: Direct Measurement Techniques with Hard-of-Hearing Children: Environment and Behavior 6(1) p. 117
N: 0013-9165
OCLC Number: 4647243973
Publication: Environment and Behavior, v6 n1 (19740301): 127-127
Database: ERIC The ERIC database is an initiative of the U.S. Department of Education.

The effect of extended contact with "normals" on the social behavior of hard-of-hearing children.
by TW Mallenby
ISSN: 0022-4545
OCLC Number: 107863896
Publication: The Journal of social psychology, 1975 Feb; 95(First Half): 137-8
Database: From MEDLINE®/PubMed®, a database of the U.S. National Library of Medicine.

The personal space of hard-of-hearing children after extended contact with 'normals'.
by TW Mallenby; RG Mallenby
 ISSN: 0007-1293
OCLC Number: 113775903
Publication: The British journal of social and clinical psychology, 1975 Sep; 14(3): 253-7
Database: From MEDLINE®/PubMed®, a database of the U.S. National Library of Medicine.

The Effect of Extended Contact with "Normals" on the Social Behavior of Hard-of-Hearing Children
by Terry W Mallenby
OCLC Number: 427052930
Accession No: EJ118344
Publication: Journal of Social Psychology, 95, 137-8, Feb 75
Database: ERIC The ERIC database is an initiative of the U.S. Department of Education.

The personal space of hard-of-hearing children after extended contact with "normals"
by Terry W Mallenby; Ruth G Mallenby
OCLC Number: 14151807
Notes: Caption title.
From: British journal of social and clinical psychology ; v. 14, no. 3 (Sept. 1975)
Description: p. 253-257.
Publisher: [Great Britain : s.n., 1975]

The missing person in measurement techniques of interpersonal distance.
by Terry W Mallenby
 OCLC Number: 678920246
Thesis/dissertation : Document : eBook Computer File
Publisher: [Burnaby, B.C.] : [s.n.], ©1975.

The Effect of Extended Contact with "Normals" on the Social Behavior of Hard-of-Hearing Children
by Terry Mallenby
ISSN: 0022-4545
OCLC Number: 4653399646
Publication: The Journal of Social Psychology, v95 n1 (19750201): 137-138
Database: ERIC The ERIC database is an initiative of the U.S. Department of Education.

Facilitating the disappearance of perceptual error to the Poggendorff illusion.
by TW Mallenby
ISSN: 0023-8309
OCLC Number: 112913792
Publication: Language and speech, 1976 Apr-Jun; 19(2): 193-9
Database: From MEDLINE®/PubMed®, a database of the U.S. National Library of Medicine.

Incidents of physical assault against child-abuse investigation workers : the nature of child-abuse protection legislation as possible reason for such incidents : some Canadian provincial examples of internal policies attempting to deal with such incidents : placing the trend of such incidents into a theoretical perspective
by Terry W Mallenby
OCLC Number: 44178037
Thesis/dissertation : Manuscript Archival Material
Publisher: 1994.

Teach your child to read : a simple method for parents and educators
by Terry W Mallenby
OCLC Number: 61554932 - 1984

The relative effectiveness of whole- and part-task simulators
OCLC Number: 222728551 – 1984

Quality assurance in medical/health care utilizing and incorporating three methods of evaluation: process, setting and outcome : an introduction to assessing medical/health care by means of a conceptual "process matrix" : with special reference to acute care and chronic care hospitals
by Terry W Mallenby
OCLC Number: 184866019 - 1986.

When the "baby-boom" cohort reaches 65 : will it be social chaos or a carefully planned transition? : an introductory research proposal
by Terry W Mallenby
OCLC Number: 184861481 - 1986.

Child abuse : a beginning social worker's understanding and use of the DSM-III-R and three reactive mental disorders following child abuse : reactive attachment disorder, post-traumatic stress disorder, and adjustment disorder
by Terry Wallice Mallenby; Institute of Psychometric Assessment (Bay Roberts, Newfoundland)
OCLC Number: 40533667 - 1994

Dealing with a violent work environment : internal policies and legislation dealing with physical assault and other threats against child protective social workers
by Terry W Mallenby; Institute of Psychometric Assessment, Applied Studies & Investigative Research.
ISBN: 0969594402 9780969594406
OCLC Number: 35875995 - 1994
Notes: Revision of author's thesis.
Description: vii, 473 leaves; 29 cm.
Series Title: Employee assistance program series.

How to make staff safe: how to reduce labour-management conflict: how to reduce staff grievances
by Terry W Mallenby
ISBN: 0969594402 9780969594406
OCLC Number: 62920434 - 1997
Other Titles: How to reduce labor-management conflict, How to reduce staff grievances

Newfoundland - The Lieutenant-Governor in Council may designate probation officers appointed under the Department of Social Services Act to act as probation officers for the purposes of this Act and may designate probation officers appointed under this Act to carry out the duties of probation officers for the purposes of the Department of Social Services Act.